CONTENTS

Forwards

I remember a Saturday morning when I was 12 years old. A spring day, mostly cloudy, but with the sun shining, and my dad and I were cycling from Appleford, the village where we lived, to the town of Didcot where we were both taking piano lessons. Appleford is mostly a mile and a half of main road lined with houses, with a few cul-de-sacs leading off from it. The roads to and from the village have arbitrary right angle bends in them as they negotiate the boundaries of local farms.

We were on the open road heading towards Didcot and I asked, "Dad, what do you think transport will be like in the year 2000?"

I was 12 years old in 1976. At that time the year 2000 was The Future. There was a science fiction comic entitled 2000 A.D. In the year 2000, I had calculated, I would be 36: at the time I could no more imagine this than imagine living as a fish.

"If things go on as they are," Dad said, "then you're sitting on it."

In the mid-1970s, the Organisation of Petroleum Exporting Countries or OPEC, as it was more widely known, had drastically increased the price of oil, and petrol prices across the Western world had more than doubled. People wondered how long fossil fuels would last, and there were confident predictions that they would run out within our lifetimes. With this set of political circumstances, my father's prediction seemed compelling, although at the time I was disappointed not to hear him talking about personal hovercraft or magnetic levitation devices.

As I write this, with the year 2000 as a fond memory rather than a far-flung future, the continued availability of petroleum products notwithstanding, my father's prediction has proved accurate. We find more oil by continually finding new ways to frack with our environment. The roads we use are more dangerously busy with motor cars, and the air we breathe more polluted with their fumes, but the bicycle is still the future.

CHAPTER ONE
London Edinburgh London

This book is about cycling. More particularly it is about cycling a long way. More particularly still, it is about cycling from London to Edinburgh and back to London in five days as part of an event called London-Edinburgh-London 2013.

I felt there was a need to write this book. Others may disagree, pointing out there already exists a perfectly good (and very readable) account of the 2009 London-Edinburgh-London event, namely Andy Allsop's *Barring Mechanicals - From London to Edinburgh and back, on a recumbent bicycle*, which any student of long distance cycling will surely have already read. However, as the title makes clear, this is an account on a recumbent, rather than a normal bicycle, and surely there is a need for a more mainstream account of this event.

Cycling is the act of riding some form of pedal-powered road or off-road vehicle, usually a bike, but sometimes a trike, very, very rarely a unicycle, and almost never anything with more than three wheels. It doesn't mean riding a skateboard, rollerskates or blades, or a scooter. The bicycle was recently voted the most important invention of all time, beating the aeroplane, the semiconductor transistor, and fire, and quite right too. It was invented some time in the nineteenth century, and more or less perfected in the 1890s with the so-called Safety Bicycle, and changed human society forever, giving everybody, as it did, affordable transport.

There are of course, different types of cycling and different types of cyclist. What to the general public is a cyclist, may be one of a huge variety. It's like beetles. There are plenty of different types of beetles. There are plenty of different types of black beetles. There are plenty of different types of black beetle about so big, and some of them look so similar that only beetle-fanciers and other beetles can tell the difference. (I might note here it wasn't Charles Darwin who said God must have "An inordinate fondness for beetles" and that quite possibly the twentieth century biologist J.B.S. Haldane didn't say it either, but somebody obviously did, even if anonymously, and there *are* a great number of species of beetles.)

So with cyclists. Children cycle. Most people cycle as children. As adults, some people cycle to the shops, which is splendid. They do it more in places like Holland where it's actually safe to do so, but they do it here as well. Some adults go further, both literally and metaphorically. Some race, some explore, some take bikes on camping holidays. Some take part in organised rides with lots of other people. Some ride regularly as part of a club, some use them to perform tricks, bouncing over street furniture in front of an audience of their peers. Some make the bicycle part of a fashion statement, riding around the city (invariably a city) with brightly coloured wheels on a minimalist machine with a fixed wheel. Fixed means you can't ever stop pedalling. Cyclists who race, explore, camp etc can do so on or off-road, or on very good roads only, or rough roads. All of these differences mean different bikes, clothing and attitude.

Long-distance cycling means riding a distance of more than about 200km (or 125 miles in old money, although the word *about* could be stretched or perhaps squashed to allow 100 miles. Riding a century counts as long distance.) In my book if you are going to call yourself a long-distance cyclist you'd be expecting to ride 200+ kilometres reasonably often, and if this is the case there are organisations to help you. Audax UK, for example, the organisation which promotes London Edinburgh London.

The word audax needs some explanation. When cycling was still in its infancy, with the first so-called safety bicycles, which used a chain and gears and could dispense with the dangerously high front wheel hitherto necessary for propelling a bicycle at any decent speed, there were cyclists busy pushing the boundaries of how far could be covered in a single day. These cyclists wished to think of themselves as *audacious* in their ambition and achievement, and thus the word *audax* was coined. The first recorded audax event was a ride from Rome to Naples, a distance of 230 km which was attempted and completed by a group of 12 riders. The idea spread across Europe, and in 1904 the French cyclist and journalist Henri Desgrange, who had already been responsible for the inaugural Tour de France the year before, published a set of regulations for the conduct of audax events. A group of cyclists formed the Audax Club Parisien or the ACP to take over the organisation of these events.

In 1920 Desgrange fell out with the ACP, and forbade them to organise. As result of this, ACP created a version of audax called randonneuring where riders were free to cycle alone or in small groups instead of altogether in one large group as was the case with the original audax ideas. The Union of Parisien Audax Cyclists was formed to run events according to the Desgrange rules. The history of these organisations, as you might expect, is long and convoluted, but the sport persists. In the UK, where the Desgrangian version of group cycling has never existed, the terms audax and randonneuring are more or less interchangeable.

The basic idea then, is this: everybody starts at the same time, or if there are lots of riders, they start at intervals; they ride together or separately, however they like, over a course of 100 or 200 or 400 or 600km or longer, following as best they can a designated route. To ensure that riders don't cheat and take shortcuts, they have to arrive at controls, places along the way where they sign in, or do something similar, to prove they were at this place at this time. At these controls they get stamps on a piece of card which acts as their proof. The card is called a brevet card. They also need to complete the course within a time limit - typically a time that means they travel at 15km/h average speed.

Quite categorically, audax is not a race. For some events there is a published list of the order and even the times that people finish, but there are no prizes. The ethos is on succeeding with the challenge, not on competition. There is usually also a maximum average speed, for example 30km/h, which is not to be exceeded; riders arriving too early at a control have to wait for it to open before they can proceed.

Most audax events are local affairs, with fewer than a hundred participants, and there is a busy calendar of them available to cyclists. There are also some famous ones which attract riders from all over the world, the most prestigious of these being Paris-Brest-Paris.

Le Petit Journal

SUPPLÉMENT ILLUSTRÉ

Huit pages : CINQ centimes

SAMEDI 26 SEPTEMBRE 1891

M. CHARLES TERRONT
Vainqueur de la course nationale de Paris à Brest
organisée par le : Petit Journal :

Paris-Brest-Paris is the oldest long-distance road cycling event in the world, with over a century of history for its 1200km.

The first *Paris-Brest et retour* was organised in 1891, before the publication of audax regulations by the newspaper *Le Petit Journal*. It was meant to be a test of the new safety bicycles' reliability and was to be a competition amongst self-sufficient riders who carried their own food and clothing. The race was won in 71 hours and 22 minutes by Charles Terront who was sponsored by Michelin and was riding with the newly invented pneumatic tyres. The race was also designed a publicity stunt for the newspaper, and as such it was a resounding success.

The next event was 10 years later in 1901, and sponsored this time not only by *Le Petit Journal* but also by Henri Desgrange's *L'Auto-Velo*. This edition of the race was so successful, particularly in terms of newspaper sales, that one Geo Lafavre at *L'Auto* suggested the organisation of an even bigger race, which turned out to be the *Tour de France*. The 1901 edition of PBP was also notable because for the first time there was a separate amateur section.

The event took place every 10 years in 1911 1921 and 1931, but the 1941 edition was postponed until 1948 due to the Second World War. The 1951 event was won by Maurice Diot a time of 38 hours 55 minutes, a record which is likely to stand for a very long time because since then there has been no professional racing event, and the course used has been on smaller roads with more hills.

The professional race suffered declining interest among riders, since it clashed with a particularly lucrative series of races that occur after the Tour de France, and both 1956 and 1961 versions were abandoned for lack of competitors. The amateur event however continued from strength to strength, with an ever increasing field. It was run every five years until 1975, and thereafter every four years. In 2011 there were nearly 6000 riders.

London Edinburgh London is the British answer to Paris Brest Paris. It was first organised by Audax UK in 1989 on a small scale. There were 29 starters and 26 of them finished. And it started in Doncaster so it should have been called Doncaster Edinburgh London Doncaster, but that's by the by. This early venture was clearly deemed a success because the event was repeated four years later in 1993 and every four years thereafter, and each year it was bigger than the last. In 2009 there were more than 400 finishers.

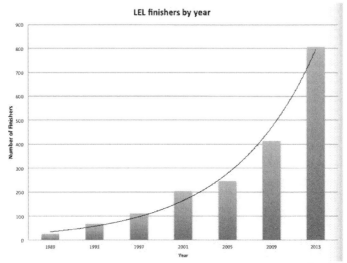

The graph shows that the growth in the event is roughly exponential, doubling roughly every five years. At this rate, there will be over a million riders by 2065, and before the turn of the century, the numbers will exceed the entire population of the United Kingdom, presumably with a very large number of foreign riders.

As soon as I heard of the event, I knew I was going to do it.

CHAPTER TWO
About the Author

As I approach the hallowed age of fifty years I might be having a midlife crisis. In fact I think I've been having a mid-life crisis since I was 30. Before that it was adolescent angst. When I'm properly old, I'll have to think of another name for it.

To be honest, a crisis is a bit of a luxury. If you are having a mid-life crisis, or a crisis roughly of the same description at any other age, it means you have time to worry about something other than starving or freezing or being hacked to death by people from a neighbouring country. People don't have mid-life crises when they have lost their job, or their wife has just left them, or their house is on fire.

More to the point, my midlife crises are often difficult to justify to My Good Lady. Nevertheless I approach 50 in the privileged position of having such a crisis.

One answer to such a life-changing problem is to spend more money. A luxury solution to a luxury condition. In my case, I decided a new bicycle would do the trick - at least until I was safely into my fifties and could find a new dimension to the midlife problem. A yacht would be a better solution, but I know from other people's experiences that you need both money and time to enjoy a yacht properly, and I don't have enough of either. Plus I can't afford a cheap yacht, whereas I *can* afford an expensive bicycle.

The bike would be the definitive bicycle. It would be custom-made, to fit my own unique shape and personality. It would be the last bike I would ever buy and it would last me the rest of my life, which I naively continue to hope will be a further fifty years. (My grandmother is 101, after all.)

This solution leads to a couple of further problems, the first of which is what bike to buy. The second is how to justify the purchase both to My Good Lady and to myself.

Before you buy a bike or a revolver or a swimming pool, it is important to know exactly what you will be using it for. In terms of bicycles, I do the following:

- I cycle to and from work, and for most other solo journeys of less than 5 miles or so.
- I cycle on moderately long rides when I get simultaneously the inclination, the energy, and the time.
- Occasionally, I ride off road through parks and bridleways and especially in the North Downs to the south of London. Sometimes I accomplish these rides with Junior and very rarely with My Good Lady.
- Very occasionally, perhaps two or three times a year, I ride a long-distance event such as the Ditchling Devil 200 km audax or the Dunwich Dynamo.

Every other year or so, I manage to go cycle camping, generally solo, except for a handful of occasions with Junior. Junior needs a great deal of persuasion for this, and will always maintain he never wants to go again afterwards, although he does actually enjoy cycling.

The best bike to ride to work, unless you have a particularly hilly ride, is a cheap and tatty looking machine which is in good condition and which has a single gear. The simpler the better. It's for getting from A to B. You don't want to spend time maintaining it, not unless cycle maintenance gives you genuine pleasure of itself rather than simply as a means to an end. And you don't want it nicked. I have a couple of bikes like this anyway. So the Dream Bike Midlife Crisis Solution has nothing to do with the cycling I do most of.

I thought about this a lot. Most of my riding was on roads and for moderate to long distances. When I cycled with others I wanted to be able to keep up with them, so a lightweight fast bike made sense. Such a bike would do for everything except mountain biking and cycle camping.

And cycle camping I do so infrequently...

And yet...

I would love to one day cycle around the world. I don't have the bottle to do it. I don't have the time while I have a job and a mortgage, and I don't have quite enough selfishness to abandon my family for a gap year. Gap years are for the young, and perhaps I should have cycled around the world instead of taking a bus tour through Africa.

I read a lot of books by people who have cycled around the world and blogs by people who are in the act of doing it. And I dream.

Because of this dream I want my bike to be capable of a journey it will probably never make. It's a funny world.

I read around the subject. Various glossy magazines, advice on websites like the CTC's, Rob Penn's informative book *It's All About the Bike.* As I read blogs by round the world cyclists I took careful note of what kind of bike they rode. Vince Cox rode a standard production steel bike fitted with a Rohloff hub. Mark Beaumont rode a heavy-duty aluminium framed bike with a Rohloff hub. Alastair Humphries rode an old mountain bike. Emily Chappell rode a purpose-built steel tourer with a triple chain set. Sarah Outen rides an aluminium frame with a Rohloff hub. Tom Allen rides a steel-framed mountain bike.

It dawned on me that if I was going to spend a lot of money on a 50th birthday-present-to-myself bicycle, perhaps I should be cycling more. Especially as cycling is good for you. It is particularly good for you if you have a predisposition towards heart disease and have too much stress in your life, as I do. It hits the cardiovascular exercise and meditation spots at the same time.

While I was surfing cycling web blogs for the ultimate bicycle, I came across a mention of *London Edinburgh London 2013* on a blog called middleagecyclist.blogspot.co.uk.

My Good Lady liked the sound of this, because it involved cycling with other people, which she considers safer than cycling on my own. This may be to do with road safety or it may be to do with mental health; I haven't discussed it with her.

I decided I was going to have a bicycle frame custom made for me in steel, and it was going to use a Rohloff rear hub, something which delivers 14 equally spaced gears in a rather neat (albeit heavy) package, without the need for derailleurs or extra chain wheels or front or rear gear mechanism. I couldn't afford the Rohloff, at least I couldn't afford a new one, but I had a cunning plan.

I'd been watching eBay. I'd been hoping to purchase a Rohloff-equipped touring bicycle for a knockdown price, but I had only succeeded in learning that such bicycles kept their resale value really well. However, in the desperate hope of finding the knockdown price I had learnt to target eBay auctions that ended at inconvenient times, and had downloaded free software that allowed me to make bids on auctions for me at those times. When a full suspension mountain bike with Rohloff came up, the auction ending at 2:30 AM on a Tuesday morning, I made my move.

I bought the bike for £800, which sounds a lot for a second-hand bike, and I have bought cars for less, but a new Rohloff hub costs more than that on its own. And here is the cunning plan. I removed the rear wheel and the Rohloff bits and refitted the bike with conventional gearing using spare parts from my garage. I managed to resell the bike for £400. I put the Rohloff gear to use on my old mountain bike, but ultimately the plan was to use it with the custom-made frame.

This was a plan that had evolved gradually. One of the more fascinating things about evolution is that it is not a particularly efficient method of doing things. The biological version results in us humans having a backbone suited for walking on four legs and suffering chronic back pain, for example, and a tailbone you can sit down hard on and hurt yourself. In terms of my organisation, it became apparent that while the custom-made bicycle frame and London Edinburgh London were both achievable objectives, they were not going to happen in the same year.

Which meant I needed another bike, since my now Rohloff-equipped mountain bike was too heavy for the event and my two other bikes are both fixies, without gears for the hills.

The lovely Welsh clothing company Howies used to sell a T shirt which bore the equation

$$X = N + 1$$

where X is the number of bikes you need, and N is the number of bikes you currently have. My Good Lady and I disagree on this sentiment, but she was the one who suggested we buy a rack to store multiple bikes in the garage, and I take this as tacit approval.

So I purchased a bicycle purely to ride London Edinburgh London, a rather elegant Bianchi. Another eBay bargain. I promised MGL I would sell this new bike afterwards, although I didn't put any time limit on this intention.

Naturally enough, you can't just buy a bike and then ride it to Scotland and back. That would be far too simple. For one thing, you have to ride it for 100 km or so to check that everything works, and that you are comfortable riding it. For another, the bike you have bought is very unlikely to be perfectly suited for the task without some minor adjustments, and thirdly, in the course of riding it you are very likely to think of some additional changes you would like. In short, the bike needs to be fettled.

Fettling is the art of making final adjustments and fine-tuning a piece of machinery to a state of perfection. Or you could call it fiddling about with your bike. I spent a lot of time doing this.

I adjusted the saddle height and handlebar height, changed the pedals and refitted handlebar tape with additional padding underneath it. Both wheels needed truing, and I needed to replace the ultra-narrow racing tyres with something a little wider and more comfortable. I replaced the chain, because you should replace a bicycle chain fairly regularly, and if you don't do this it wears out more expensive components. I added minimalist mudguards, because otherwise when it rains, I have learned from experience, my arse gets wet and then it becomes very sore. I found these weren't minimalist enough; there wasn't enough space around the wheels to fit them, and so returned them to the shop and bought an even more minimalist design of mudguards at double the price that *did* fit. Then I needed lights.

All in all, this bicycle spent many hours on the work stand in my garage, while the garden needed weeding and the bathroom needed repainting.

You are supposed to do some training. In order to enter Paris Brest Paris you have to complete a number of shorter long-distance audax rides; this is to ensure that all the riders are physically up to the challenge. With LEL there is no such compulsion, but there is an expectation that you get yourself fit enough.

I normally ride to and from work five days a week, which comes to a distance of just under 100 km per week. In addition, once or twice a month I might ride a longer distance, perhaps 100 km in one day, all of which probably makes me significantly fitter than the average British adult, but not remotely fit enough for LEL. I needed to do something about it.

I started riding round Richmond Park. There's a good mountain bike route along a boggy lane through Wimbledon Common to the park; one circuit of the off-road track there and back makes 25 km of fairly demanding hilly riding.

In the spring and early summer I rode on a number of rides with Simon Legg's Friday Night Rides to the Coast group. The rather wonderful FNRttC meet at Hyde Park Corner at midnight on Friday evenings and then cycle at a reasonably leisurely pace to a seaside location to enjoy breakfast. Halfway through the route, there is generally a stop at a church hall or similar, where Simon has persuaded some local volunteers to sell us tea, sandwiches and cake at 3:30 in the morning. I have always found it a refreshingly otherworldly experience to cycle in a large group of people in the middle of the night. Realising that I had to harden myself up, I started cycling the return journey on the Saturday mornings instead of taking the train. Or at least I attempted to, generally making it at least half way home before finding myself outside a station ready to quit.

I entered some audax events. The idea was to do a couple of 200km rides, then a 400km ride, this being a distance that takes up most of a weekend, with 24 hours or so on the bike and the rest of it travelling to and from the start and then recovering from the trauma, and finally I wanted to ride a 600km audax. If I could do that I would definitely be able to set out for Edinburgh with confidence.

Sadly, a brief look at the calendar told me I couldn't do a 600, or at least I couldn't do one before July 27th. The closest such events were in Dorset, or in Wales. I would need to spend some time sleeping during a 600, and wouldn't be able to complete it in less than 48 hours. Factoring in a journey of at least two hours before, and two hours after the event, and also factoring in that I work as a schoolteacher, and being sleep-deprived and standing front of a class of Year 10s who do not necessarily share my passion for physics on a Monday morning was not a good plan.

Meanwhile, I rode the Hop Garden 200k event, so called because it is in Kent and they grow hops there. I rode this on a fixed wheel and suffered severely on the hills - at one point having to get off my bike and walk, fortunately without witnesses. That was when I decided I needed a different bike. Two weeks later, and riding the eBay Bianchi, I rode the Stonehenge 200, which began in Elstead in Surrey and went west into Wiltshire, passing close to the eponymous stone circle, but much to my disappointment, not affording so much as a glimpse of it. I found the new bike quite exciting, and was childishly riding away from people on the uphills, enjoying more gears than I could find a use for, but scaring myself on descents, where the dented front rim vibrated ineffectually against the front brake blocks, and finding the ultra thin racing tyres and pothole combination more uncomfortable than I wanted to put up with. Hence some of the fettling.

On a Fridays ride to Brighton, at half past three in the morning, in Horley, a village just to the north of Gatwick Airport, I met a woman wearing a Paris Brest Paris cycling jersey. She was slightly-built, and in her early 60s, but she had clearly been cycling all her life. I asked her about long distance events.

"It's a fantastic experience," she said. "Paris Brest Paris is wonderful. You should do it."

I told I was doing LEL in July and I was worried about my fitness.

"If you want to do it, you'll do it," she said.

I told her I was doing lots of long rides, but I wouldn't be able to do a 600.

She said, "The important thing is to ride on a Saturday and Sunday." Apparently there is a significant difference between doing two long rides with time between them to recover, and doing two long rides on consecutive days without that recovery period. You need to train the body to cope without it.

"Thank you," I said.

In mid June I had booked myself on what would have been my only 400 km ride before LEL, but unfortunately a few days before the event the organisers had to cancel. It seems there had only been six entries. Instead, I signed up for the Ditchling Devil 200 on the Sunday, and decided I would ride at least 100 miles on the Saturday. During the week, I sat in front of the computer and plotted out a ride that would take me out into the South Downs to Midhurst and back, giving me plenty of practice at climbing hills.

The Ditchling Devil is a relatively new audax ride with the marvellous USP of starting within 2 miles of my house. The route takes you to Brighton via Ditchling Beacon, a steep hill notorious by virtue of being on the London to Brighton charity ride, when thousands of non-cyclists suffer on it, and takes you back towards London via the Devils Dyke, another steep rise on the South Downs. It also takes in some of the steeper hills in Surrey, including Coombe Lane, which by coincidence I had tackled the day before. The PBP lady's words found resonance with me because on the second day the same hill was very much harder. Whereas two weeks earlier on a new (to me at least) lightweight racing bicycle I had been singing up steep hills, now in the same places I was suffering. I also discovered a use for the very lowest gears on a triple chain set.

Riding into the wind towards the summit of the Devils Dyke, I could see two riders in the livery of Dulwich Paragon, one of the larger cycling clubs in south London. They had been a hundred metres or so in front of me for quite a while and I'd been thinking that if I could catch them up it would be easier to cycle with them than to fight my way through the wind on my own. I had been entirely unable to catch them up, but then at the Devil's Dyke National Trust viewpoint its was necessary to stop and take note of the word BIKE printed on a laminated sheet of A4 paper to serve as proof you had indeed cycled to this point. So I did catch up the Dulwich Paragon riders and having done so asked if I could cycle with them.

They were good guys to cycle with, not only because they were friendly, but David (I think that was his name, but I'm guessing here) was a big strong guy who was happy to sit on the front taking the brunt of the wind and large enough to give significant shelter to somebody cycling behind him, and Alistair was also signed up for LEL, so he and I spent quite a bit of the rest of the ride chatting about our preparations and/or lack of them.

My summer holiday began at the end of the first week of July, giving me three weeks to make final preparations. There was still some fettling to be done, but the most important work was on preparing my body. More training required. On the following Thursday, it was my grandmother's 101st birthday and I wanted to be there in Bristol for that.

Grandma had recently moved out of the townhouse where she had lived for the last 30 years into a rather lovely retirement home that overlooked a playing field where she had played hockey matches as a girl. I set off on the Tuesday morning, shortly after MGL and Junior had gone to work and school respectively. I was cycling out of London during the latter part of the rush-hour, but going against the flow it wasn't too bad and soon enough I was moving through rolling countryside on a sunny morning. I set off too fast, wanting to prove to myself that I was getting fitter, instead merely proving how unprepared I was. I needed to stop for a second breakfast in Newberry, and sat on a convenient set of sunlit stone steps outside a Co-op eating two croissants washed down with a pint of chocolate milkshake. By the time these carbohydrates kicked in, however, I was warming to the task, feeling stronger as I went. I noticed the wind was blowing the wrong way, giving me a tailwind when it is supposed to come *from* the south west.

I had an unnecessarily sudden meeting with a white van in Marlborough as I was cycling through the town centre. The white van in question pulled out of a parking space around the edge of the Market Square, giving me almost but not quite enough time to slam the brakes on and avoid hitting him.

"Didn't you see me?" Sadly, this is an all too common starter to a conversation between a cyclist on the motorist.

"Yeah," the young man said, thoughtfully. "I thought you would have been able to stop."

During the collision, I had had time to brace myself, and I had hit the broad side of the van with my shoulder. Fortunately I hadn't done any real damage to myself, but unfortunately, although I must have made a very loud bang, neither had I managed to put a dent in the van.

The latter part of the ride towards Bristol was along the old A4, the wide smooth tarmac now almost redundant as far as motor traffic was concerned since it ran parallel to the M4. It was something of a treat to have such a quiet yet good-quality road pointing almost directly in the direction I wanted to go. From Bath to Bristol, the last ten miles or so, I cycled along the old railway line that became the very first Sustrans path in 1979. It was the latter part of the rush hour when I was riding here, and it was cool to be sharing the space with so many cyclists, most of them clearly commuting home from work, some of them out for a training ride, heading out for open country.

I arrived in the right part of Bristol around about 7 o'clock. My uncle met me at the door to the home.

"You're just in time for the Tour de France," he said.

A word about my uncle. He is called Trikin Dave, partly because his name is Dave and partly because he rides a tricycle. It is possible that he is the reason I got into cycling in the first place and therefore how I came to ride London Edinburgh London and then write about it, and in consequence one reason you are reading this, but it is certainly why I could be sitting on the floor in my grandmother's room in the old people's home watching TV with her, my uncle, his long-suffering wife, and my parents, still wearing my sweaty Lycra.

Because of my uncle, nobody in my family is especially impressed with any ridiculous cycling achievement I might manage. When, at the age of 17, I first cycled to visit my grandmother, she wasn't especially surprised and neither was she worried when I hadn't arrived at 7 o'clock in the evening having confidently predicted I would be there by five, because he'd done all this when he was 17.

My uncle is best described as an eccentric (weirdo has negative connotations). Not only has he spent much of his life cycling ridiculous distances competitively as well as non-competitively – his favourite being the annual Mersey Roads 24-hour time trial, he also keeps bees, despite being seriously allergic to bee stings, needing to carry an EpiPen with him to provide him with intravenous adrenaline in an emergency; he runs a community cinema, and produces a photographic blog. He has a peculiar sense of humour understood by few outside our immediate family, and is a talented argumenter. He holds an enormous number of unusual opinions and will argue in favour of them enthusiastically. One of my favourites is that traffic lights make road junctions both less efficient and more dangerous. Six months after a triple heart bypass, he achieved almost 300 miles on his tricycle in 24 hours, so clearly cycling 800 miles in five days on only two wheels whilst in decent health, and 20 years younger was never going to be an unrivalled achievement in my family.

After Tony Martin won the time trial stage of the Tour at Mont St Michael, I spent a further half-hour drinking more tea and catching up with my grandmother's most recent news before the five of us who didn't live in the old people's home went out for pizza that Grandma paid for. Here I put an appetite gained over seven hour's cycling to good use. We went back to Grandma's house, which my mother and uncle were arranging to sell, and spent the night there.

The following day we spent mostly at the old people's home, Grandma's new address, where the staff had put on a party in her honour complete with party hat and cake. I think the home was quite proud of its newest and also oldest resident. Grandma milked the attention and thanked the staff and her "fellow inmates" afterwards for making her feel so welcome. It was a lovely occasion, one well worth cycling 200 km to attend.

On the way home, my uncle accompanied me as far as Bath, riding the trike he had ready for the forthcoming 24-hour race. He chose to do this wearing a bright red Dennis the Menace cycling jersey, very short blue Lycra shorts and a pirate bandanna under his helmet. It's great fun cycling with my uncle, something I've not had much chance to do since he lives in Edinburgh, and I live in London. En route to Bath I appreciated the way he could manoeuvre the unwieldy looking trike, particularly along the Sustrans cycle path, which is periodically enriched by the kind of obstacles designed to prevent people using motorbikes on the route whilst being merely infuriating to its primary users. I learnt there is a measure called a standard pram width favoured by councils and the builders of footpaths etc, and that most footpaths were designed to permit the movement of a standard pram. His trike was a standard pram width so it was in theory possible to negotiate pretty well any footpath, let alone cycle path, riding it.

Having enjoyed the meteorological anomaly of a tailwind while cycling westwards towards Bristol, the same unusual weather conditions gave me a headwind on the way home. Having had a full rest day to recover, as well as birthday cake, it wasn't too much of a problem and I arrived before MGL and Junior were home from their day's labours.

The Sunday before LEL was the Dunwich Dynamo, one of my favourite events. The Dunwich Dynamo is described by Wikipedia as a semi-organised through-the-night ride. It has been going about 15 years, and tradition has it that it started with a group of bicycle couriers on a Friday night deciding as they left the pub that they would cycle to the seaside. Presumably they chose to ride with a following wind since I can't think of another reason why you would choose the seaside in Suffolk when Sussex and Kent are so much nearer. The ride is 120 miles long, which is 200 audax kilometres more or less, and goes from a park in London Fields to the town of Dunwich on the Suffolk coast, always on the Friday night in July closest to a full moon.

Dunwich itself is little more than a village, but once upon a time it was the capital of the kingdom of the East Angles, and up until the 13th century was one of the most important ports in England. Its demise since then has been due to coastal erosion. On New Year's Day in 1286, a large storm swept most of the town into the sea and caused silting of the River Dunwich which made the port less favourable for shipping. Further storms in February and December of that year compounded the damage. The harbour was finally destroyed in a storm in 1328 and 20 years later another storm swept 400 houses into the sea. Pretty well every building that was present in the 13th century has been destroyed by storms or flooded by the sea since then. The remains of eight churches in the town rest under the waves, and, perhaps not surprisingly, there is a legend that on still nights you can hear their bells ringing. Whilst the palest shadow of its former self, Dunwich possesses a wide pebbly beach from which fishing boats are still launched, and a very large café next to the beach which does a roaring trade on the morning of the Dynamo.

By the time of the Dunwich ride, I had fitted a front wheel dynamo to the Bianchi, so the ride gave me the chance to test it. It was a cloudy night, with no sight of the moon but with a fierce tailwind, and I arrived at the beach just before sunrise. I had been looking forward to some early morning sunbathing and a bit of a swim, but unfortunately, in the middle of a particularly warm and sunny July, the morning was overcast and chilly. I used this disappointment as an opportunity to start cycling home, cycling as far as Ipswich before I caught a train to London.

Alongside the preparations for man (in my case) and bike, there is also the paperwork and the logistical planning. A great number of hours needed to be devoted to these causes.

It started with some simple calculations along the lines of

$$1415 / 12 = 118 \text{ hours}$$

and

$$118/24 = 4.9 \text{ days (call it 5)}$$

and then

$$1415/5 = 285 \text{ kilometres per day (which sounds doable)}$$

Further calculations involved the speed I thought I could comfortably average during a day's ride, which I was confident would be at least 20km/h, and the length of time it would take me to do the day's allotted distance, and I was happy that if I could cycle for 14 hours in a day, then allowing a couple of hours for eating and other necessary bodily functions, I would have about 8 hours a night to sleep. With some organisation, I wouldn't actually need the lights, although I considered it prudent to take them anyway.

Red tape is online these days. (Mostly) gone are the days of BLOCK CAPITALS and signing your name inside the little box, and writing really carefully because if you made a mistake you'd want to go back to the post office to get yourself another copy and start all over again. It's quick and efficient, and most of the time your efforts don't disappear into the ether for no reason at all. Entry for LEL 2013 was online. Easy. The only catch was that it started at 3 o'clock in the morning on January 5th, which required a small amount of dedication to remember. I got the feeling that as there were only 750 places available at the time (later increased to about a thousand) that demand would exceed supply, and that to wait for a sensible time in the morning would be risky.

In retrospect it seems a sensible manoeuvre for the organisers to make one criterion for entry that you have at least enough inner strength to be awake at 3 a.m. on one Friday evening in January, a cheap and cheerful way of separating the idly curious from those who were sufficiently dedicated that they might successfully complete the event.

Once registered, and with £219 on the VISA card, I shortly had access to the "rider area" of the website, where I could request where I wanted to locate two LEL-supplied bags, in each of which I could place up to 5kg of goods. I also had the option to buy a specially commissioned LEL 2013 jersey, which of course I took up.

The next stage of the logistics involved the purchase of a cheap AZ atlas of the country which I cut into convenient pieces to go in my handlebar bag's map case. I had a lovely time one evening with a highlighter pen marking the route, up and down the country. After that I started planning my sleeping stops.

Then there was the decision about what to take.

Good advice for any kind of trip that involves carrying your own kit is this: pack what you think you need. Then unpack it, put half of it aside, and pack the remainder. If necessary, repeat this process more than once. Unlike previous travel arrangements I had made, there was no need for any kind of non cycling-specific clothing. Neither was there any need for a book to read, since there wasn't going to be time for reading, any more than there would be time for hanging out in the evenings in casual clothing. Since I was carrying every item up and down gradients all day every day for five days, I was pretty clear that some extreme minimalism was required. It came down to this:

- 5 pairs of cycling shorts (no more, but certainly no less!)
- 5 cycle jerseys
- 3 pairs of socks
- One pair of cycling mitts
- One under-helmet hat
- Glasses
- Helmet
- Cycling shoes
- Waterproof cycling jacket
- Cycling tights
- Armwarmers (these are wonderful inventions. Like the sleeves of a sweater but without the sweater. They are sort of elastic and stay on your arms without rolling down very much.)
- Phone (another wonderful invention. Holds maps, music, meditation guidance, allows access to the internet, including Facebook, and you can make phone calls)
- Bike spares (two spare tubes, repair kit, multitool, pump)

It might be noted that, while this seemed minimal to me, a majority of riders seemed to require significantly less, particularly in the way of clothing.

The final admin part was a requirement to register for the event in person on the Saturday before the start. This was at Davenant Foundation School in Loughton, North East London, where the event officially started.

Davenant Foundation School has a long history, having been founded in Whitchapel in the East End in 1680 for the education of 40 poor boys, subsequently taking in 34 poor girls, and gradually growing in numbers to about a thousand; it then became a school for boys only, moved out of London to its present location in the 1960s and became coeducational again. Very little of that history was apparent during the holidays when the school was empty of pupils and staff, and it looked very much like any other 1960s school building.

Being physically there made sense because that was when you brought your maximum 10kg worth of goodies to put into the two cotton drawstring bags - mine were a pink one printed with the word Pocklington under the LEL 2013 logo, and a green one labelled Brampton. This was where I also picked up my brevet card and my free LEL water bottle.

The other reason for being physically there the day before was that at least the organisers could be confident that the riders had a better than average chance of being able to find the location on the big day.

I was warned that the following day there might be queue for water to fill the water bottles, and it would be a good idea to arrive with water in hand. I took this advice on board.

CHAPTER THREE
Before We Start

There was a prologue. It was free to enter. A 30km ride across London from Buckingham Palace to the official start point at Loughton. The Mall would be closed to traffic. There would be police escort. If the organisers had gone to all this trouble to arrange it, it would be rude not to take part. That's what I thought, anyway.

The start time was 6:00am, which in itself isn't a big deal. If you are going to cycle and do nothing much else but cycle for five days, what's one early morning start to quibble about? And 6:00 am on a Sunday morning in August is a good time if you are going to cycle through the middle of London.

We were asked to be there fifteen minutes early to allow for a photoshoot. A photoshoot sounded good. It would be nice to be in such a picture. I could almost imagine such a picture up on a wall somewhere, challenging friends and family to find my place in it somewhere. A picture for me to remind myself of the faces of the interesting people I would meet.

What I didn't really think about the 6:00am start time, now 5:45am, was the lack of sufficient public transport to get me to the Mall for it. My preferred option would be a train to Vauxhall, and a quick ride over the bridge and up to the palace, but the first train didn't get me to Vauxhall before 6:00.

Without the train, there would be a 20km prologue to the prologue. More to the point, because I'm nervous about getting lost, I would want to allow myself plenty of time, which meant leaving the house by 4:30. And I'd need 15 minutes to get up and dressed and have a bowl of cereal. I told myself it was all part of the unique experience and didn't think of it again until the night before the start.

Given that sleep, and getting enough of it, would be an important factor in the ride, I wanted to be decently rested before the start. An early night and no alcohol would be the order of the evening, or at least an earlyish night, and a moderate amount of alcohol. Unfortunately, I'm something of an insomniac, and the excitement of the ride ahead of me, together with the knowledge I'd need to be awake for a quarter past four in the morning, made the prospect of a good night's sleep a poor one.

In the event I got off to sleep quickly enough, or must have done, as I can't remember trying to sleep. I woke up half an hour before the alarm, and lay awake and warm in my bed until the alarm was ready to ring and then I cancelled it so MGL didn't have to wake up too.

I was in stealth mode in the kitchen, drinking juice and eating cereal as I got dressed in full night-visibility cycle kit, when MGL came down to wish me good luck. Knowing how she feels about her bed and not wanting to leave it before dawn, particularly in the first week of the holidays, I was touched by this.

It was just getting light as I stepped out of the house and made my way to the garage. The bike was ready, fully fettled, the saddlebag and bar bag loaded with their carefully selected sets of items, the bottles - one water, one expensive isotonic mix - were ready in their cages. I used to keep bottles ready in the fridge the night before a big ride, but then I also used to go half a mile down the road and have to do a U-turn because said bottles were still in the fridge. By the time I'd wheeled it around to the gate, turned the GPS on and given it a minute to find itself on the surface of the planet, and I'd put on gloves, helmet and cycling glasses, MGL had had time to get a camera ready. The photo was staged, with MGL standing half way up our road in her dressing gown as I came out of the drive and rode purposely towards her.

It's quiet in London at 5 o'clock in the morning, but not that quiet. There was enough traffic that I had to wait at some of the red lights. Every cyclist has their own rules about red lights. There are some who ride through them whatever. Some of these have sufficient agility and speed that they can survive almost indefinitely, even in London. There are those who refuse to ever disobey the Highway Code believing it to be unethical. Some will proceed if it is clearly safe to do so, and if they are not going to inconvenience any other road user. My own rule is that I won't go through a red light unless it's both safe and there's nobody looking. I rarely break that rule, and never do so at the lights outside the school I teach at. I don't want to set a bad example. At 5 o'clock on the morning of Sunday 28th July 2013 it was busy enough I stopped at a half dozen red lights and it would have been eight if I hadn't broken my rule.

I was breaking the rules especially as I got closer to the Palace because it was looking more and more as if I would be late. As a rule of thumb, wherever I'm going, and whatever I'm going to be doing when I get there, I arrive not-quite late. I believe psychologists have an expression for this. On the plus side, it means I'm rarely bored waiting, but on the minus side I usually end up stressed. MGL also has an expression for my habit of arriving not-quite late.

I live in London, albeit 12 miles from the centre. I cycle everywhere. But I have a poor sense of direction and haven't cycled to Buckingham Palace before. I was using the GPS to help me get there with a minimum of stopping to look for directions. Nevertheless, I managed two wrong turns, which might not be considered the greatest of omens at the start of 1400km of cycling.

I arrived bang on 5:45 in front of the Palace. I stopped because MGL had asked me to take a picture of the notice of Prince George's recent birth. The notice had been removed, purely for my inconvenience, but on close inspection there was a bunch of flowers a well-wisher had left, so I took a picture of that. Obligation done with, I rolled towards the congregation of cyclists a hundred yards down the Mall.

And I waited. There were hundreds of men and women and bicycles milling around, waiting for some kind of start. There was an atmosphere of excitement and confusion. It was an international crowd, with many languages being spoken or represented on riders' clothing, and many varieties of skin colour and hair style. The name plates on the bikes had riders' countries written on.

Most of the crowd was English, or at least British, and while those who had flown distances to participate in the event talked in loud voices or took photographs, we Brits rarely speak to people without first having got to know them, so most people there were standing astride their bikes, looking around, soaking up the atmosphere, but not talking.

By 6:00 there was no photograph nor yet a start, but that was fine because there was no hurry and, even if you had nobody to talk to, it wasn't raining and the atmosphere was interesting. I enjoy people-watching on such occasions. So many types of person, clothing, bicycle, mannerisms. And cyclists are more interesting than non-cyclists, anyway.

And soon enough there was a woman talking to us with a megaphone, there were a couple of people wearing yellow bibs positioning themselves to stop the traffic.

"Could everybody put their bikes behind the white line there?" the woman's amplified voice said. The white line she pointed at was at the traffic lights behind us.

Some people did. Others were too busy chatting, or they didn't understand English, or they couldn't be bothered. Or they realised it was unlikely that several hundred riders were going to fit neatly across two lanes of traffic by the lights.

A tripod rose in front of us, a camera on top of it already two metres off the ground and inching its way upwards. More and more riders moved into the space in front of it. Order prevailed. Wise words were spoken. Photographs were taken, and there was cheering.

And we started. Hundreds of riders rolling unsteadily forwards along the Mall towards Trafalgar Square.

There is a very loosely organised protest group called Critical Mass that aims to increase awareness of cyclists. It is probably structured in a similarly ad hoc way to *al Qaida*, but with more laudable objectives. Critical Mass rides occur in many major cities around the world, usually on the last Friday of the month, and the idea behind them is that there are so many cyclists present in the same place and at the same time that they take over the whole road, dominating the traffic to the extent that it is not possible for cars to overtake and the road slows to the pace of a parading bicycle. My nearest Critical Mass events in London begin at about 6:30pm underneath Waterloo bridge by the South Bank Centre.

The metaphor comes from nuclear physics. Fissionable isotopes like uranium-235 and plutonium-239, while they are stored in small amounts, are relatively safe. When a large enough quantity of the isotope is assembled, the aforementioned *critical mass*, then a chain reaction of fission events (fission is the splitting of the atomic nucleus, which produces, among other things, particles called neutrons which are capable of causing further fission events) will occur. An atomic bomb is detonated by using explosives to push a number of small pieces of uranium or plutonium together so that a critical mass comes together in a fraction of a second; the fission chain reaction spreads through the whole quantity of nuclear fuel, releasing huge quantities of energy all at once in a devastating explosion. The cycling equivalent is less dramatic, and more benign.

300 cyclists, starting at the same time from the same point in central London constitute such a critical mass, especially early on a Sunday morning. They quite naturally and automatically dominate the traffic. Moreover, it only takes a few individuals, perhaps only one, to jump a red light in such circumstances, and the whole critical mass of cyclists does the same, demonstrating the same flocking motion as sheep or birds or fish. When a large enough number of cyclists pass through a junction - and it takes a decent interval of time for this to happen, perhaps half a minute - then motorised traffic will wait. What is remarkable is that nobody seemed to mind. I didn't hear anybody honking a car horn. Most drivers were visibly interested in the phenomenon, and most of the cyclists were reasonably polite, thanking the public for their patience. It warmed the heart. Possibly those who drive through the capital at six o'clock on a Sunday morning are not overly in a hurry.

We cycled, and, as we cycled, the critical mass spread out along the road, dissipating a little, so that the situation more closely resembled normality. Once the mass was no longer critical, as a light went red in front of riders, they came to a stop. After a mile or so, traffic rules were accepted again, especially towards the back of the group, where the cyclist density was lowest.

Once moving, it is easier to talk to other cyclists. It seems more natural to chat when you are riding beside another person. "Nice morning for it, isn't it?" or "Is that a fixed wheel?" or "Where have you travelled from?" all seemed to work. Perhaps its something to do with the fact that you can cycle alongside somebody for a while without talking and it doesn't feel awkward, so that there's no pressure to talk. Perhaps there are psychologists who have written theses on this.

The route took us off The Mall onto Birdcage Walk, before turning left in front of Big Ben and taking us along Whitehall to the Strand where we turned east. We followed the Strand and then Fleet Street, the route of the A4.

After a couple of miles I met Alastair from the Ditchling Devil ride. I hadn't seen him since then, but he was easy to spot in his smart blue Dulwich Paragon kit. I wasn't sure if I remembered his name but it was printed on the card fixed to the black carbon frame of his bike.

We got talking. Neither of us had done as much training as we intended to. He'd been knocked off his bike by a women in a hatchback the week before and was glad to be a) alive, and b) well enough to start the ride, which made him more accepting of some physical pain, some visible damage to his bike, and the feeling that he probably wouldn't be able to complete the event.

We were chatting happily, and enjoying the sights of London. I appreciated that some of the foreign riders were stopping to take photographs. It never fails to give me a good feeling to see tourists taking photographs of the city I live in. It's a reminder of something I might otherwise take for granted.

We went east on Cannon Street to Monument, where the A3 begins, and along Monument Street and up Pudding Lane where the Great Fire of London began nearly 350 years ago, and then back in an easterly direction on Eastcheap and then Great Tower Street. At this point the extra 2 litre bottle of water I had brought, that didn't quite fit into my saddlebag, made its push for freedom. How long it spent inching its way out from the cover flap of the bag I don't know, nor do I have a clear idea of how long it waited, hanging over the back wheel, before it jumped. But jump it did.

The bottle hit the road with a loud enough thump I knew something had happened, and when I turned to look behind, I could see the bunch of riders behind parting, flowing either side of the rolling plastic cylinder.

I put the brakes on, and came to a stop, and realised the bottle was rolling down the road towards me, much to the amusement of everybody watching. It then rolled past.

I followed it, then rode alongside, while it made steady, albeit sluggish, progress down the street, managing perhaps a hundred yards before it tired of the effort and stopped outside the Hung Drawn & Quartered Pub, now ready to accept a ride attached to the saddlebag once again.

Alastair had waited for me, and now we were at the back of the bunch, following others onto the A11 along Whitechapel Road and then Mile End Road, traffic rules definitely applying. Out of the centre, the road was less scenic perhaps, interesting in terms of the geography of East London but not something the tourists would be photographing.

We turned off the A11 and passed the extended site of the London Olympics, inevitably remembering the previous summer's highlights. I never got to the Olympic village, regrettably, and still haven't got closer than cycling past it. We went uphill towards Stratford, (the one in Essex), detoured around it, and continued upwards towards Epping Forest and on to Woodford and then Buckhurst Hill, which is where both *Essex Wives* and *The Only Way is Essex* were filmed. From there it was only a couple of kilometres to Loughton.

Loughton was a fair distance, and it took over an hour and a half of stop-start cycling, and another catch-the-bottle session before we got there. The town is scarcely part of London at all, but at least it is within the bounds of the M25.

CHAPTER FOUR
Actually Doing It

At Davenant Foundation School, the second time in 24 hours, we followed the signs to the bike parking, past a large plastic water dispenser where nobody was queuing. I locked my bike because I had a lock and because I was going to be here for a couple of hours.

The school dining room was now full of people and expectation. An enormous queue snaked across it, and we had to step out into the hall to find the back of it. Obviously the very worst time to join a queue for breakfast would be when the prologue ride has just arrived, but with nothing remotely pressing to do besides have a hearty breakfast, we ended up standing in the line.

A lot of cyclists, mostly in bright colours, tight clothing, hobbled around on cleated shoes. There were groups in matching kit — six guys from Finland in blue here, a group of Poles in red, a bunch of blokes in blue shirts advertising 34' Nomads. Alastair waved to a small group in his Dulwich kit. There was a big guy with a TV camera - I later learned this was the filmmaker and cyclist Damon Peacock - a big furry microphone poking out of the side of it, and he was interviewing a man dressed like a cartoon Frenchman, striped shirt and beret. Another man I noticed wore a cycle jersey with #bloody cyclists on it.

Once I had my breakfast, including my tea, I joined the Dulwich cyclists for a while. Only Alastair and Sam were doing the ride, and the others were well-wishers. Alastair didn't expect to see Sam after the start, because Sam was going to finish in 72 hours, possibly before Alastair had got to Edinburgh. Sam was like that.

Alastair and Sam disappeared shortly before 8:30. I had at least half an hour to kill before I needed to head towards the start line. I chatted to a slightly-built pale young man who had sat down opposite with his plate of toast.

Where have you come from? For some reason, despite a lack of identifying lettering on his yellow jersey, I felt he was from somewhere overseas.

"From Russia. Siberia."

"Wow! You've come a long way."

"Yes. Is my first time outside Russia."

"Very brave. What's cycling like in Siberia?"

"Is very difficult. You can only cycle half the year. In the winter there is snow."

I didn't catch his name, and although he started the same time as me, I didn't see him again, so I assume he was one of the fast riders, like Sam, and finished days before I did. I hope so. It made the ride seem more special, that there were people investing so much time and money to come and ride it. Made me feel lucky it started on my doorstep.

I wandered around. I drank from the two litre bottle of water that had bounced and rolled part of the way, leaving my water bottles untouched. Fifteen minutes before my allotted start time I stood in front of my bike in the bike parking facility and cleaned my teeth. I would have done this in a washroom like a civilised person but I left my minimal wash kit in the handlebar bag and I had left the handlebar bag on the handlebars.

While I was thus engaged, two guys standing adjacent to nearby bicycles were putting on suncream and simultaneously comparing their own wash kits.

MAN1: That's a huge kit! What have you got in it?

MAN2: Only the usual things.

MAN1: Go on.

MAN2: Toothbrush, toothpaste, shaving stuff, suncream, Sudocrem, deodorant, shampoo

MAN1: Deodorant! What are you doing? Are you planning on going out in the evenings or something?

MAN2: No, I just . . .

But Man2 didn't finish his sentence as he noticed both his friend, and myself, giving myself away as an eavesdropper, were laughing heartily.

MAN2: I can tell by your reactions I've made a *faux pas* there, and I apologise.

Sun-tan lotion application complete, Man1 and Man2 got on their bikes and set off for the start.

I followed them around the front of the school buildings on a course defined by temporary barriers that eventually corralled a small group of us into a waiting area, about ten metres square. People were waiting, standing astride their bikes, perhaps a little nervously, chatting, and looking at their watches. I looked at my watch and it was already a quarter past nine.

At that point a man stood at the front of the waiting square and spoke to us, something about enjoying the ride, about it being the seventh occasion of the LEL and other such things. There was also something about a London to Cambridge ride that would be sharing some of the same roads out in Cambridgeshire.

And then we were off.

As Confucius said, the longest journey starts with a single turn of the pedals. There was a strange juxtaposition of the ordinary, the ordinary being cycling with a bunch of other people along a wholly unremarkable wide suburban street with wholly unremarkable sleeping policemen on a sunny morning, and the extraordinary, which in this case was the knowledge that this was a cycling journey of 1400km.

Although I'd already cycled 50km that day, this was the beginning. I went slowly, a relaxed pace, keeping up with the people alongside me, but not trying to catch anybody up the road. I had been worried about going too fast at the beginning, and burning myself out, so I was consciously doing the other thing.

Any route starting in Greater London is going to be plagued with traffic lights. There are approximately 6000 traffic lights distributed over a network of about 9000 miles of road, so you might think that, on average, travelling in London, you go about one and a half miles before meeting a traffic light. It's probably worse than that, because many of the roads without traffic lights are residential streets you would avoid if you were actually trying to go somewhere. There seemed to be a traffic light every half mile here.

As a result, the fifty riders in the 9.15 group were quickly spread out over a mile, then two miles. I caught a glimpse of Man1 and Man2 at one point, but they were riding away from lights that were turning red as I approached. I stopped and watched the man with the deodorant and his friend disappear into the traffic. I never saw them again, and as with the man from Siberia I can only hope they had a successful ride.

We crossed the M25. The M25 is where London finishes, as far as I'm concerned. If I go for a ride and don't cross it, I haven't been out of London, in which case I haven't really been on a ride. Sure, there are bits of green that might fool you into thinking they are countryside - Riddlesdale, Epping Forrest, whatever, but they are not. They are inside the M25, forever imprisoned by a ringfence of three or four carriageways of tarmac in either direction.

Gradually suburban became countryside. The traffic lights thinned out. I headed north.

There is a school of thought that says before any big cycle ride, you should get your bike set up right at least a week early, and then not meddle with anything at all for that week. You should ride a hundred or so miles with the new chain, the new brake blocks, the saddle at the height you have decided, and the handlebar bag mounted where you want it. Like many helpful bits of advice, it is the sort of thing you remember after the event, when it becomes clear in hindsight how beneficial it would have been to have followed it.

I did get the mudguards on, the revised, second-choice mudguards about a week before the event. I fitted the dynamo front light at the same time, but then I didn't really get a chance to ride any significant distance in the last few days. If I had done, I would have noticed that the front mudguard had a tendency to shift itself gradually to the left until it rubbed on the wheel. Doubtless, encountering such an irritating phenomenon, I would have given it some consideration, and perhaps I would have come up with a solution. In which case I might be typing this now with ten fingers instead of only nine.

Without the traffic lights, the average speed went up, and my cycle computer was showing 25 and sometimes 30km/h. Without so many buildings, the wind became more apparent, a roaring tailwind which rewarded every cyclist with a magical turn of speed you could pretend was entirely down to your own fitness. We were motoring out of London and into the Fens, where the total lack of hills made the wind more and more beneficial.

I'm a shy person, and it takes me a while to strike up conversation and to make acquaintances even among fellow cyclists. Knowing this, I often make an effort, commenting on the weather, or on the strange church tower in the distance that appears to be leaning over at an angle, or even asking a fellow cyclist where they have come from. I usually try this sort of thing when I've been cycling next to somebody for a good quarter of an hour.

I started chatting to Steve, who was riding a Genesis Croix de Fer, which is a bike I had seriously considered buying. That was how I started the conversation. The name of the bike translates as Iron Cross, which is a German Military medal awarded for valour in the field of battle between 1835 and 1918. The British-made diamond frame bicycle is named like this because it is proudly made of steel, rather than anything more new-fangled like aluminium or carbon fibre. And there is a multilingual pun on *croix* in that it is designed as a cross bike - cross meaning cycle-cross, which is like motocross but for pedal bikes rather than motorbikes, and where competitors usually end up carrying their bikes on the steepest, muddiest parts of the course. I wanted one as it's got a hub gear and a road frame but as a cycle-cross bike a certain go-anywhere facility. Vin Cox had recently broken the round the world cycling record on one, accomplishing the task in 163 days, 6 hours and 58 minutes for a total of 18,225.7 miles in August 2010. (Alan Bate then broke the new record, albeit with a support team, in an astonishing 107 days, and this is now the Guinness World Record to beat.)

Steve had set off at the same time as me, his rider code beginning with an R. When we got chatting, what we chatted about was how many riders with an S code, riders who had started 15 minutes after ourselves, had passed us so far, and how many riders with codes beginning with P or even N (there didn't seem to be any Qs) we had passed, and which number was the greater. The S numbers that went past us tended to be in groups, young men on carbon fibre race bikes working together. The Ps and Ns were couples, or older riders. Sometimes you passed them when they were stopped at the side of the road. There seemed to be roughly the same number in either category.

After a while I was getting annoyed that my mudguard would occasionally start rubbing against the front wheel. There was no reason for it as far as I could see. I had after all got the wheel trued up so that it didn't wobble. It seemed to be true, as far as I could tell while actually riding the bike. Because the mudguard wasn't actually screwed down to the bike, but attached by elastic bands and clips, it could be moved with careful bending or pressure from one side. I tried doing this, carefully lest I get my fingers caught in the spokes, which is always a painful experience.

I think I did this at least three times before I did actually catch my fingers in the spokes. Ouch! I immediately thought that was stupid, and I had my finger in my mouth, sucking the pain away.

When I looked, there was no blood at first. Relief, even if it still hurt.

A couple of minutes later there was blood. But not much.

I was thinking what an idiot I was. What I didn't manage to consider was *why* the mudguard was moving into the wheel. Apparently it's quite common to make a silly mistake, and while you are thinking how silly you are, you carry on making even sillier mistakes. When I play chess I often play idiot moves right after I have just played an idiot move. In fact it was a further four days before I thought to wonder why the mudguard was moving into the wheel, by which time I was at the end of the ride. If I'd thought about it, I would have realised that the front light wiring, wrapped around the mudguard stay, was putting a constant pressure on the mudguard, which, being unfixed, would gradually move into the wheel. If I'd thought about it, I could have rerouted the wire going to the light, and the problem would have been solved.

But I didn't. In any case I had already broken my finger, but I wouldn't realise that for a couple of months.

When I stopped for a pee, Steve didn't, and I never saw him again. This is like life, meeting people and leaving them behind, or them leaving you behind. We constantly meet new people, and we leave old people behind. Or are left behind ourselves.

There was blood seeping from my finger whenever I took it out of my mouth, but it wasn't flowing fast enough to drip anywhere, and now that I didn't need to pee, I wasn't really feeling the pain. I was feeling more pissed off that Steve didn't wait for me than anything else, and over the next couple of miles, more pissed off still that I didn't manage to catch him up either.

By now, we were mixing with the London to Cambridge crowd. Now, I must admit to a bit of snobbery here. London to Cambridge is 60 miles or 100km and it's flat. It's a gentle day's ride. Although at this point in the day, the Cambridge cyclists had travelled just as far as I had, I felt superior to them. I have to confess that. It's humbling.

The London to Cambridge ride was hundreds of men, women and children, most of whom probably were unused to cycling more than five or ten miles at a go, enjoying a lovely day's ride and raising money for charity (Breakthrough Breast Cancer) at the same time. Most people don't cycle stupid distances on a routine basis because they have other things to do with their lives. That's my humble pie done.

The point is, the happy cyclists gently heading for Cambridge were in no hurry. It was a lovely day, everybody was riding with the wind behind them, they were making good time and they were at this point nearly halfway there. They were going slowly, and there were lots of them. I was going relatively quickly, and needed to overtake them all, making sure there was nothing coming the other way in the way of motor traffic every time I did so. And I still had this idea of catching Steve up so I could have somebody to talk to.

I didn't need to talk to Steve. I just wanted some company, but it had to be company that was travelling at the same speed as me. I didn't want company enough to dawdle and find myself running behind the schedule. At the back of my mind I was already beginning to think that schedule might prove to be harder than I gave credit for.

The other danger was that I followed riders to Cambridge and missed the turn off. Already we'd passed one place where our routes separated, and a steward had been happily shouting "For Cambridge turn right! For Edinburgh straight on!" Now we had rejoined.

And while I was worrying about missing the turn I missed the turn. Because I was worried, I was trying to read the route sheet and check I was going the right way. I can't read a route sheet while I'm cycling, but I was trying to anyway. It was because I was so reluctant to stop riding to work out where I was that I went wrong. When I stopped cycling to read it properly I got the feeling I'd gone wrong, and then after five minutes faffing with my iPhone to get Google Maps, I could confirm that I had indeed missed a vital side road a mile back.

A thing about Google Maps, and using it while out cycling, is that any place you are in need of a map is more than likely to be remote, and therefore you are more than likely to be waiting a long time for a weak phone signal to allow you to download the relevant map page. So I waited. Another thing about using Google Maps when you think you have made a wrong turn on a country lane is that you are likely not to be in a good frame of mind to be waiting. Or perhaps that's me. Certainly I'm not one to think, let's find a nice shady place to sit down, have a sip of water, and perhaps open a packet of dried fruit to nibble on while I'm waiting.

I retraced my tracks. The dozens of London to Cambridge cyclists going the other way all nodded and greeted me warmly just to annoy me more, and then I had to wait for a break in the continuous stream of happy cyclists so I could make the turn I'd missed and cycle north and leave them behind.

There was a young guy standing with his bike by the road, I asked him if he was okay.

"Maybe," he said, uncertainly. He had an Italian accent.

I stopped. He was mending a puncture. He had the front wheel off and had removed the tyre, and he was looking anxiously at it.

"What's up?"

"Do you have something for a hole?"

"I've got a puncture repair kit," I said. I was surprised that somebody could be cycling 1400 km and not have a puncture repair kit.

"No, I have this. I need something for big hole."

He showed me. There was a circular hole in the outer tyre, about 2 mm in diameter. The tyre itself was not in great condition. It was a thin racing tyre, well worn, and he should have replaced it the previous week. On the other hand I thought he would get away with the hole, for a while, provided the inner tube was repaired. Certainly long enough to get to the control where somebody might be able to help him out with a new tyre. I told him this, but he wasn't happy.

Another cyclist stopped. An American perhaps in his early 60s, with rimless spectacles and the air of an academic. He was very soft-spoken. "You need a tyre boot," he said. "Normally I carry one."

A tyre boot is a short length of tyre, perhaps a fragment of a worn-out one you have saved for the purpose. If there is a split in your outer tyre, the tyre boot can be put inside and can reinforce the repair. The American was looking through his tool kit to see if he could find anything suitable. I was continuing to persuade the young Italian that he would likely be able to cycle another 40 kilometres.

"Oh, I know what would do it," the American exclaimed, and he produced from a pocket a set of business cards. He handed one to the Italian. "If you fold that inside the tyre it will work for a while."

"What's on the card," I asked. He showed me one. It had his name, and the legend Long Distance Cyclist where you might expect the name of his company.

"When I meet somebody on a ride, I find it much easier to give them a card than look for a pen to write an address down." Unfortunately I didn't take one of his cards, unaware at the time that I was going to be writing this, and now can't remember his name.

The first stage finished at St Ivo School in St Ives in Cambridgeshire, a huge modern comprehensive school. I thought St Ivo was a typo on the route sheet but it was there on the sign outside the entrance too. There were also temporary barriers to guide you to the control, and an arrangement of the same kind of barriers to act as bike stands where you could lock your bikes, or simply lean them there if you were confident nobody would take it. I noticed there were signs on the way out for both London and Edinburgh.

As at Loughton, the school was staffed by squadrons of volunteers in red T-shirts, all of them smiling. The first half dozen of these lovely people pointed me in the direction of the control, where three more volunteers sat behind a desk busy with piles of paper, a couple of laptops, and coffee cups. The paper was mostly lists of the thousand riders. At the control, I gave my brevet card over to be stamped, and while that happened my time thus far was recorded online and on the relevant sheet of paper next to my name and rider number.

To enter the school dining room we were requested to remove our (cleated) shoes. Cyclists being, by and large, and despite what some in the media might suppose, polite people, there was an enormous spread of cycling shoes, neatly paired up, lined up along the corridor leading to the dining room.

Soon enough I was fortified by tea, and working my way through soup, bread and a plate of pasta.

On the wall I noticed a poster bearing the words of the famous rhyme, in a child's hand:

As I was going to St. Ives,
I met a man with seven wives,
Each wife had seven sacks,
Each sack had seven cats,
Each cat had seven kits:
Kits, cats, sacks, and wives,
How many were there going to St. Ives?

I'd always thought the rhyme referred to the more famous town in Cornwall, but now realised it wasn't necessarily so. St Ives in Cambridgeshire, which was once St Ives in Huntingdonshire after it was Slepe in Huntingdonshire, was always a thriving market town and therefore you could expect to see people carrying sacks of things on the roads towards it. Personally, I suspect the anonymous author of these words only chose St Ives for the rhyme with *wives*, and didn't care very much about the geographical location.

The answer to the puzzle works out to be 2800, or is glibly given as 1 (the narrator) but a case may also be made for the answers 0, 2, 7, 9, 2753 or 2802. Really.

I was joined at the table by a large man with a jersey that identified him as Finnish. He looked very hot. I asked him how he enjoyed the first stage.

"It's okay," he said, with less than infectious enthusiasm. "But too fast. I am cycling with a group. We average over 30 kilometres per hour to come here."

The record shows I took six hours to cycle the 99 kilometres from Loughton to St Ives, an average of 16.5km/h. Allowing that it was probably 103km I travelled, and that there might have been as much of an hour of time actually stationary, adding all the traffic lights and other junctions, the stopping to urinate and taste my own blood, and the waiting for Google Maps, it's still only only a tad over 20km/h.

"That's fast," I said, for a moment feeling rather inferior. To change the subject, I asked him what Finland was like for cycling.

"It's not so good. Unlike in London, the drivers are not expecting you. They think you should not be on the road. Here is much better to cycle."

I told him I was surprised to hear that.

"Also, you can only cycle for half the year," he said.

CHAPTER FIVE
Strange Worlds

After drinking tea and eating and drinking tea, I changed the map in the sleeve on top of my handlebar bag and checked my Facebook account and then I used the facilities, and finally I found my shoes and went out to the bike. I turned the GPS back on and fixed my handlebar bag and then rooted through it to find the soluble isotonic drink capsules I would dissolve in my drinking water to make it more appealing. Then I took my water bottles back towards the control where there was a giant plastic water vessel on a table just outside the door, and I filled them. I got back to the bike, unlocked it, put my helmet and track mitts on, and finally I was ready to hit the road again. It was just gone four o'clock and I'd been at St Ivo school for nearly an hour.

I was cycling on my own again. I passed slower riders every few minutes or so, but only very occasionally would somebody faster than me fly past. I reflected on this for a good while before I concluded that most of the fast riders had already passed me, either on the road or while I was dawdling in St Ives, while slower riders would be ahead of me for a lot longer, since most of them had left before me in the morning.

On my own, and riding at my own pace, I wasn't going especially fast, but it was consistently over 25km/h. At this rate, my planned itinerary would be entirely reasonable, and I would get a decent night's sleep each day and still make the pace.

You don't notice the wind when it's behind you. Or if you do, you don't give it much significance. It's quiet with the wind in your direction, it's quieter than if there were no wind at all. Quiet is easy to forget about. And you prefer to think it's your

49

muscles doing all the work, rather than give credit to something as invisible as the air itself.

Likewise, the problem with the wind going the other way, is that you can't give yourself the credit for conquering something that you can't see. If you can't see it, it's not there. Unlike a great mountain pass, which, when surmounted, gives you the unrivalled view that is both reward for your efforts and an acknowledgement of them, riding into the wind is just hard.

But I wasn't riding into the wind today and it wasn't hard at all. I heard other riders talking amongst themselves, mentioning the wind. Somebody said "It's a fantastic tailwind!" and I thought it was a comment I wouldn't have made.

Somebody else said, "The weather forecast is for it to be calming down later in the week."

Suits me, I thought.

In my head I was simultaneously dismissing one man's opinion as not being particularly significant, whilst taking another's comment on the same subject as very good news. If the wind would choose to blow me all the way up to Scotland, then fantastic, but I won't be mentioning that to my friends, and if the same wind fails to oppose me on the way home, so much the better.

I continued with 25km/h on my way north, passing people who were going slowly, being overtaken by those faster. At some point I hoped somebody would come past doing 26 or 27km/h and then I would join them, riding in their slipstream.

In the meantime the Fens were flat and uninteresting.

I say they were flat. The road north from London into Cambridgeshire isn't hilly by any means, but roads don't get much flatter than in the Fens. Ten kilometres into this stage, we passed the ironically named village of Ramsey Heights, famous for a rather wonderful nature reserve that, needless to say, I didn't stop for. Ramsey Heights is at an altitude of two metres, according to the map.

When I say they were uninteresting, don't get me wrong. I don't wish to offend, and I do want to sell this book in

Cambridgeshire and Norfolk as well as in London and Lothian. The Fens make a fantastic landscape, one that has been heroically claimed from, and held against, the sea over generations, but from a bike they do appear uninteresting.

The road is flat. In the distance there is the next village, the next town. To the sides there are electricity wires, telephone lines, and beneath them, the dykes that channel the all-important water that keeps this land alive.

If you got off your bike and went down to the water you would see the marvel of straight lines of water, channelling the rivers to irrigate every inch of farmland, you would see the culverts and the weirs and the valves and the pumps necessary to keep it all in order. If you paused awhile, you would see the birds stalking fish in that water, you would see the ripples of voles and otters swimming. You would sense the marvels of engineering, and the patience of the natural world.

Whistling through on the bike, keeping to a pace, unwilling to waste the gift of speed when there were so many miles ahead, all there was to see was the flat land, the pale green of drying grass verges, the blue of the sky, the white of the clouds in the enormous sky.

Flatland is the name of a short novel written by the headmaster and theologian Edwin Abbott Abbott in 1884, and this is a topic that popped into my head on a hot day while I was riding without company. (Abbott's parents were both called Abbott, and they were cousins, which is offered as some explanation for the man having two identical barrels in his name.) The full title of the book is *Flatland: A Romance of Many Dimensions,* and it was written as a satire on Victorian culture, and particularly the class system. However its enduring fame wrests with its exploration of a two-dimensional universe, its comparison with our own three-dimensional one, and contemplation of worlds with more than three dimensions. As such it is still celebrated to this day, particularly amongst those who enjoy either science fiction, or maths or physics. But it is an awesomely funny book, one that hasn't dated at all in the 100-plus years since it was written.

In the two-dimensional eponymous Flatland, all people are strictly two-dimensional. Their every movement, their bodies, their whole lives are contained in a two dimensional plane. When they see their fellow creatures, all they see is a line, and only by the way that line changes by rotation, can they infer the shapes of others.

But the shapes are important. In Flatland the social satire aspect is achieved by a strict class system: the highest classes are circles, or multisided people who are close to being circles. The professional classes, including the hero, are squares. The hero, A Square, was originally the author's pseudonym. The working classes are all triangles. And women are simply lines.

A three dimensional shape, a sphere, visits A Square in the course of the story, and outlines the possibilities of a higher dimensional world. Together they visit a one dimensional world where the only person is a dot who makes up the whole universe. This dot is impossible to talk to, because he cannot perceive of any being existing outside himself. If A Square or the sphere say something to him, the dot perceives this as his own idea. A Square accepts the possibility of the third dimension, and imagines a four dimensional world is also possible, something the sphere is unable to accept. When Einstein's ideas of Space-Time became currency twenty years later, the book Flatland enjoyed renewed interest, which has never died away.

Its probably just as well that before long I met up with somebody I could ride with and had a conversation to interrupt the daydreams.

Ed came past me at exactly the right speed, greeting me with "How do?" as he did. He was a big bloke in bright lycra and a red complexion. I caught onto his wheel (this means I followed closely to benefit from his slipstream, rather than putting my hand on rapidly rotating pieces of metal, of course) and found I could keep up. I rode behind him for a while and then drew level on a slight rise where it was easy for me to do so. Since he was heavier than me, as the vast majority of men are, the incline gave me an advantage.

"It's not like back 'ome, this," he said. His accent was from Yorkshire. Presumably the rest of him was too. I think his name was Ed, but when he told me, it was one syllable while we were riding, and I wasn't sure if I got it right. He had a blunt face to go with a blunt way of talking. When I saw him later in the day I noticed he was ginger, but this, his most obvious feature, was entirely hidden by a helmet when I met him.

"How are you doing?"

"Not so bad. Making up for lost time." Ed's event number showed he'd started half an hour before me.

"Where did you lose it?"

"Faffing aboot."

"Easily done," I said. "Where do you think you'll get to today."

"I've got a bag at Pocklington."

In Crowland, part of the so-called South Holland district of Lincolnshire, a group of boys enthusiastically told us to go left at a T junction. But they were barely able to suppress their giggles, so it wasn't difficult to believe Ed's assertion that it was a right turn according to his GPS. Nevertheless, I found my place on the route sheet as I followed.

The next command was

SO @ stgd X (by monument)

which means straight on at a staggered crossroads. The monument was a very odd, inordinately bulky piece of stone that looked more like a building than anything else, although a building without doors, windows or indeed apparent purpose. A hundred yards up the road there was a Spa where Ed pulled up and announced he was buying a drink, and I decided to wait for him.

I still had a bottle of water with me, after half the stage covered, and had no need or desire for any form of purchased liquids. If I'd thought about the three bikes leaning up against the wall I'd have known there was a queue inside and that I'd have had time to wheel back and have a good look at the monument, although, I'm not sure I would have bothered. I didn't, so I won't write any more about it here, leaving it for another page.

Two cyclists came out of the shop and claimed the two bikes parked there. Both were wearing *yacf* jerseys. The online forum group "*yacf*" was well represented. In addition to a number of *yacf* jerseys, there were also a number of riders with, in addition to the LEL labels on their bikes, a much larger *yacf* label that indicated their *yacf* moniker. These usernames were generally self depreciating, and often mildly amusing, with examples like *Pieeater*, *Red Lantern Pete*, *middle-aged cyclist*, and *Pickled Hamster*, only one of which I just made up.

Online forums are something of a mystery to me. Many people, and not just cyclists, spend a lot of their time in such a forum. Forums can be very useful; a forum can be a magnificent facility if you are in need of very obscure and specialist information. They are a brilliant way to organise meetings, cycle rides, protests etc.

Nevertheless, browsing through the directories of most forums takes you to a very alien place peopled by beings with names like *pickled hamster*. In a forum like *yacf*, there are threads, that is conversations or the equivalent of conversations, which just go on and on, long after they have ceased to serve any useful function. For example, a thread that begins with a question about cycle helmets is may produce two or three suitable answers in a short space of time and yet continue, with three dozen contributions from five or six different people, gradually drifting off-topic until it becomes a discussion of cakes. Godwin's Law of Nazi Analogies says that eventually all forums will involve Nazis or Hitler. With cycling forums, eventually a topic will, with some certainty, end up with a discussion of cake.

A typical thread might go something like this:

NewGirl: Can anybody tell me what the brightest available dynamo front lights might be?

Fast Eddy: Lots of people swear by the Edelux.

fashionmista: IMO the supernova is way better. It looks cool too.

Marxbros: Before you worry about the merits of one or other very expensive lighting system, you might be better off considering what you want the lights for. Do you need to see where you were going, or do you have some need to impress?

fashionmista: The supernova is way better than the Edelux.

PoorDarling78: IMHO you can get a perfectly good battery LED front light for 20 quid. Why spend 100 pounds?

Fast Eddy: You might spend £20 on a battery front light. You can spend the spare £80 on the decent helmet you will need when you crash because you can't see where you are going. Anybody who thinks decent lighting is a luxury is an idiot.

Marxbros: Anyone who spends £100 on a light has too much money.

Fast Eddy: Roger, if you went out and got yourself a job, instead of wasting your life and everybody else's time delivering your opinions online, perhaps you would be able to afford a decent bike.

Marxbros: We can always rely on you, Pete, to make things personal. If I had a job like yours I could be a wanker instead of a cyclist.

Ilovelucy: spend money on expensive cycling toys, and don't ride. Or ride, spend money on cake.

PoorDarling78: we like cake!

Carloss: I h8 nazis who wanna dictate how u spend yr money

To be fair, I have a tendency to exaggerate. It is very rare for an online conversation to go all insulting and shouty, but they do tend to go off at tangents. If you are sufficiently middle-aged not to know what is meant by acronyms such as IMO, then the excellent (and frequently amusing) online urbandictionary.com can be very useful.

(As a footnote, both the Edelux and the Supernova are perfectly excellent lights, And I wish I could justify spending the money on either. I saw lots of people on LEL with one or other of them, and nobody I asked regretted the purchase. If either manufacturer would like to get in touch with me and give me an example of their products to test, then future editions of this book might present a more detailed account of their merits, and perhaps an exclusive recommendation.)

The danger with threads drifting off topic, is that after a while, somebody says something that upsets somebody else, who in turn replies robustly enough that the first somebody is also now upset, and the thread becomes more heated. In a recent edition of *New Scientist*, there is a discussion of the way people behave when they can remain anonymous. Pickled Hamster is more likely to insult you than Daniel Malcolm.

People who post abusive contributions are known as *trolls*.

Mike Godwin introduced his law in 1990, writing that, "As an online discussion grows longer, the probability of a comparison involving Nazis or Hitler approaches 1." Of course, taken literally, the premise cannot fail to be true, since if the discussion becomes infinitely long, it will contain every possible combination of words, every possible sentence, and every idea, including nazis, Hitler, and a troop of monkeys writing Shakespeare.

Godwin introduced his law as an experiment in memetics. Memetics is the study of memes, which are ideas or phrases that are part of our culture, and which mutate and evolve over time. Godwin has said that although he phrased the law in the same way that scientific laws are phrased, his purpose was to get people who glibly compared someone else to the Nazis to think a bit harder about the Holocaust.

The word *meme* was invented by Richard Dawkins in his book *The Selfish Gene*. The word is a conscious half-rhyme with gene, and Dawkins was interested in applying the ideas of evolution to ideas as well as to living organisms.

The expression *on your bike*, meaning *go away*, is a meme that became enormously popular once it was used as a repost to the conservative politician Norman Tebbit, who had said, in the course of a speech about unemployment, that when his father was out of work, he got on his bike and went to look for work. The website *barackobamaisyournewbicycle.com*, which creates a random sentence about the US president each time you log onto it, may be responsible for the *is your new bicycle* meme, where "your new bicycle" is a new reason for excitement in your life. Compare *is the new black*.

yacf.co.uk has grown large enough that its influence extends beyond cyberspace to the real world, as evidenced by the range of *yacf* cycling gear on display during the ride. In fact in many ways, *yacf* is like a traditional cycling club, with (albeit unofficial) club runs and other events, organised online. As a club, it was by far the best represented of any club for LEL2013. But its somewhat peculiar name belies its history.

yacf stands for *Yet Another Cycling Forum*, which was started by people disenchanted with *Another Cycling Forum*. Enquiring about the historical reasons for this disenchantment is opening up a can of worms. There seems to be a great deal of animosity between these two websites; something that reminded me of *The Life of Brian* and the feud between the Judean People's Front and the People's Front of Judea.

I believe that *another cycling forum* was started up by people after the online forum of the magazine *Cycling Plus* was suspended due to the number of trolls inhabiting it. Presumably the quantity of abusive contributions appearing on the *Cycling Plus* website forum was not a good advertisement for the magazine.

Personally I'm not so sure about the fashion of using an alias on these forums, however I didn't want to stand out at different, so my username at yacf is *The Thin Man*. I don't use forums very much, but when I do it's usually to look up if somebody has reviewed a piece of kit or has news of a particular event. It is very rare for me to post anything I have written myself. People who only read the contributions of others in forums are known as *lurkers*.

For the record some other useful cycling forums are:

CTC forum - CTC Forum • Index page
BikeRadar - Forums - BikeRadar
Cycle Chat - Cycle Chat
Single Track World - Singletrack Forum

There was a lot of activity on yacf in the months leading up to LEL, and there is a permanent forum devoted to the event (you can find it through the audax forum there). Personally I used the Facebook page more often rather than yacf simply because the Facebook page had pictures.

The two *yacf* cyclists rode off up the road as Ed came out with a bottle of coke and an ice cream. Other cyclists arrived while he was consuming this. Setting off again after fully fifteen minutes, there was now a small group of us. We went North along the River Welland and its associated channels and banks and dykes. After a while I noted a church poking its spire up above the horizon.

To be fair, a church does not need to be so very tall in Lincolnshire to be proud of the horizon, and any such can be seen for a very long way. As we approached this one, it quickly became clear that not only was it the tallest landmark around, but that it was also leaning over.

I put on some speed to level up with Ed and mentioned it to him. He grunted, but without much interest. After a moment I drifted back behind him and got on with cycling. Over the next few minutes I watched the spire growing gradually larger. By the time we entered the village of Surfleet, whose church possesses this spire, it was clear that it really does lean. Checking my facts, it leans by some 5 degrees from the vertical. A little more than the more famous Tower of Pisa, which only manages 4 degrees. It began to lean very shortly after it was built, 700 years ago, and despite huge buttresses added to shore it up in the 15th century, it is still moving.

Leaning church towers are apparently not all that rare in Lincolnshire, where the soft soil is prone to subsidence. In the wonderfully named village of Dry Doddington the church tower leans at 5.1 degrees to the vertical; there is talk of this Lincolnshire village becoming a tourist attraction due to its church's world-record breaking leaningness.

From Surfleet we travelled up through Spalding and Gosberton and numerous smaller villages in a land of rivers, heading for Kirton.

Which sounded a grand place to me. I expected a town with a striking and probably very old church, but on arriving, hot and tired on a very warm day, it seemed to be merely a large village with little to make a striking impression. Nevertheless, Cherchetune, as it was originally known, features in the Doomsday Book and was where the first kings of Lincolnshire were crowned. I don't know much about the history of the kingdom of Lincolnshire so I'll stop there. The church of St Peter and St Paul is undoubtably old, but it was "dismantled' in 1804, apparently with the aid of gunpowder, and then rebuilt, largely with the original stone. Kirton became a prosperous market town, and Thomas Middlecott founded a Free Grammar School there. After that Kirton became an unprosperous market town, and then a village without a market. The school no longer exists, but a modern school, named after Middlecott, serves the area, and this is where the control for LEL 21013 was situated. The school is appropriately located on Edinburgh Drive.

CHAPTER SIX
What it Does to You

My first priority at Kirton was the toilets, which was to prove a place of great interest and learning. I was thirsty after another three and half hours in the saddle, but I needed to make space for the liquid I planned to take in.

Drinking lots of water, like wearing a sunhat and lots of sun cream whenever you go outside in daylight, and wearing a lifejacket if you go near the water, is one of the ubiquitous suggestions of our time. There is an idea that schoolchildren cannot think adequately unless they drink several glasses of water every day, and that everybody puts their kidneys and liver at risk if they are not adequately hydrated. Like much well-intentioned advice, there is some truth behind it. The problem is that the idea you should ensure you don't become dehydrated has become the instruction: *drink more water!* The idea that, whatever the circumstances, drinking an extra glass or bottle of water will help. The fact that there is a multi-million pound industry based on selling bottled water may have something to do with it.

People have died, particularly during marathons, through drinking *too much* water. We should take everything in moderation. (Including moderation, as my uncle might say. He's not a big fan of moderation.)

On the other hand, on a hot day, while engaging in continuous exercise, taking in enough water is genuinely a problem. And people die of dehydration too. (Especially in hot nightclubs after taking Ecstasy.)

Pinned to the wall above the urinals was a set of A4 laminated posters about dehydration and its dangers. Most strikingly, there was a colour chart for you to compare your urine against — basically the darker it was, the more serious your dehydration. For each shade of yellow there was advice for what you should be doing. For a few moments I wondered if this was a school notice, something for the boys to check for themselves at lunchtimes on hot summer days, before I realised if that were the case there would surely be some clever comments written on them. Not to mention illustrations. The colour of my stream was borderline dehydrated, and the poster gave me the advice to keep drinking liquid and be careful not to let myself become more dangerously dehydrated. Tell me something I don't know, I thought.

I met Alastair again in Kirton. He was just finishing his meal when I entered the school dining hall carrying my tray, and he called me to join him. Soup, pasta, tea. It had taken me 8 hours to catch up the half hour head start he had on me. He didn't think he was going to finish due to his ongoing soreness problem as much as the aching body parts after his crash, but he was also mindful that the further he rode, the more it was going to cost him in rail fare back to London.

"You'll make it," I said. He didn't strike me as the sort to quit. At the time I was naive enough to think that very few people actually quit once they'd committed themselves to such a ride. We agreed to set off for Market Rasen together.

"I'll meet you out at the bikes," he said. "I've got to lube up, first."

I'd never heard of Sudocrem before. Junior never suffered from nappy rash so it never entered my vocabulary as a father. I'd never really had a problem with saddle sores, either. I'd had a sore bum once after cycling to Brighton and back - the longest ride I'd ever done before LEL - when it had rained and I'd been unprepared and without mudguards. It wasn't much of a problem because I didn't ride any further than work and back for the following week, and although there were sore bits, I didn't suffer with them overmuch through five miles each way. I used a bike with fat tyres and a soft seat for a week. By the following weekend things in the pants department were back to normal.

LEL, I knew would be different. It was the riding on consecutive days that was going to be a problem. I'd had a chat with my uncle about it.

He mentioned Sudocrem. I wrote it down, getting him to spell it out to me. "You can get it from Boots."

"Thanks," I said.

"It's worth spending money on shorts," he added.

I told him I had been.

"I get more of a problem with pubic hair."

"Oh, I said. I felt that was more information than I strictly needed.

"I don't have a lot of it, but it can get in the way."

I think he said it got in the way. I was trying not to listen.

"I don't get on with shaving, but the hair removing cream I find works well."

"Thanks for that."

This was of course long before my initiation. By the time I'd got even as far as Kirton, I was less delicate about discussing such matters.

I filled up my water bottles from a picnic table outside the entrance bearing very large plastic water containers. I filled one bottle with water and one with water mixed with salty fruity powder. I took these back to the bike, fixed my handlebar bag in place, then found my tub of Sudocrem and made my way to the gents. I wasn't sore yet, but I was being preventative.

There was a large queue inside the gents, snaking around the confined space in front of the stainless steel urinal wall and the two sinks and ending by the cubicles. There were two men using the urinal and reading the information about urine colour but when they had finished, nobody left the queue to take their places. There was a man in front of the sink reaching deep into his shorts with one hand.

"I got this heat rash last weekend," the man was saying.

"That's nasty," somebody replied.

"It's on my upper body as well," the man said, and, having finished inside his shorts for now, he lifted his cycle jersey to show a line of angry red marks across his very white chest, like a sash. A rash like a sash.

"Ouch," was the sympathetic response.

"It's the same in the saddle area. I don't know how far I'm going to get. Just put the cream on and hope for the best."

"All you can do," were the words of wisdom.

The man put another two fingers full of white cream somewhere inside his shorts, then washed his hands, and put the tub into one of his jersey pockets. Once he was gone, I took my own tub, and, much more covertly than was probably necessary, applied a little cream to that small stretch of skin between bollocks and arsehole. When I was done, I had a pee, using the other hand, then went to the sink.

By the time I was finished, Alastair was walking towards the water table with his empty bottles so there was no immediate hurry to leave.

From Kirton at five o'clock in the afternoon, we turned right, following a hand-posted sign towards Edinburgh, along the aforementioned Edinburgh Drive. Soon enough we were out in the strong tailwind and the late afternoon sunshine and zipping along as if there really wasn't very much to cycling to Edinburgh and back.

The landscape remained completely flat; very much a foreign landscape to me. I thought I grew up in a flat part of the world, this being Oxfordshire, on the edge of the Downs but not in them. I never needed to change gear cycling to school at any rate.

But Lincolnshire, like Cambridgeshire and Lincolnshire, and for that matter Suffolk and Norfolk (which remain beyond the scope of this book, although they may be dealt with in later volumes should an unexpectedly lucrative publishing deal come my way), are flat.

The foreignness continued with the names they had for things here. We cycled along the North Forty Foot Bank for example, through villages which called themselves Toft Tunnel, Hedgehog Bridge, Holland Fen, Dogdyke.

The North Forty Foot Bank was beside a small water channel, and it does lie to the North of South Forty Foot Bank, but it was by no means forty feet in height, and well beyond forty feet in length - it went on for a number of miles. The Toft Tunnel didn't have any signs of underground activity. Hedgehog Bridge held no structure of any kind for crossing a body of water, but a little research has secured the information that there was at one time indeed a bridge, and that this bridge across the channel had a metal frame with spikes resembling a hedgehog. The same source tells me of a Hedgehog Bridge School that seemed a splendid institution for its 100-odd year history between foundation and demolition. Holland Fen I wrongly thought gives away the engineering origins of so much of Fenland, and Dogdyke was once called Dokedyke; I have no idea what the Doke part is about, but it probably isn't anything to do with dogs.

The flat landscape continued towards Woodhall Spa, which has a minor tourist industry based largely on the mineral springs that were discovered in 1811 by one John Parkinson who had been attempting to find coal. John Parkinson had spent several thousand pounds in his attempts, which were finally abandoned when his 300 m deep shaft was flooded by the spring water. And some 25 years later the local lord of the manor decided that the spring was an asset, finding that the water was rich in iodine and bromine, and he built the spa baths and the Victoria Hotel, which were the centre of the industry until the well collapsed in the 1980s. From Woodhall we passed through Horsington, which may or many not have had something to do with horses, and Minting - whose claim to fame is that it is a Thankful Village, one without a War Memorial to the Fallen of the First World War because it was lucky enough, and presumably very thankful indeed, not to lose a single life to that conflict. East Barkwith may have had something to do with dogs or indeed Dokes, but probably didn't.

I don't remember all that much about these 68km to Market Rasen, which took a little under 3 hours. Alastair and I arrived just before dark, debating about whether or not to continue to Pocklington or to call it quits and spend the night here.

Market Rasen, once called Rasen and on the River Rase, is a small town of 3000 with a large comprehensive school of over a thousand pupils, which was used as the control. This was where I very quickly decided to spend the night. It was an easy decision. My schedule told me I needed to arrive here by 9pm and be setting off for Pocklington within the half hour, or sleep here and be off by 8 in the morning. My schedule was the one that assumed I could average 20km/h over each stage, and have the luxury of 6 or more hours sleep each night. But I didn't like the thought of arriving for a night's sleep at 2 or 3 in the morning, since the next stage was 84 km and even my naively optimistic schedule said it would be three and a half hours. I also guessed that with so many other riders also aiming for Pocklington, and only 250 beds there, that I would very likely not find a place to sleep.

I checked on the bed situation at Market Rasen before I queued for my tea and soup and pasta. There were beds. There was a procedure, but I was able to book one as long as I was going to be using it in the next half hour.

I told Alastair my plans. He agreed on the night's sleep, but wanted to get up much earlier. I believe he said something like 3 o'clock, but my brain shut off these details.

"I think I'll wait until five."

"You'll catch me up anyway."

"Yeah," I agreed. At some point in the day.

We ate quietly, seriously, methodically. We refilled tea cups and ate unreasonable quantities of cake. I excused myself and phoned My Good Lady.

To bed. A volunteer in a red T-shirt checked my name against a large sheet of paper with names in a big grid.

"When do you want to wake up?" he asked.

"Oh." I was a little surprised by the question. "About five, please."

"Five?" He sounded equally surprised at my choice.

"Please," I said, making an effort to sound confident.

Six, he wrote, in one of the spaces on the grid. Then I saw him write a code on another sheet of paper against the time 0500.

Another volunteer in another red T shirt led me down a half flight of steps to a darkened school gymnasium, leading the way with a torch.

Now, everyone knows what a school gym looks like. A big open space, with climbing bars or something technical on the walls. Lines for various ball sports marked on the floor. You probably played basketball or volleyball or netball or badminton in a school gym. You almost certainly did exams in one, with little desks marked out in rows, a hundred or more young people sitting in regulated silence.

As a school teacher I have other associations with the gym. Namely walking up and down those rows of desks, watching young people do those exams, the occasional assembly, and inept amateur five-a-side football on a Friday evening.

I'd never slept in one.

As my eyes adjusted to the dark, I could make out rows of rectangular shapes, beds this time not exam desks. Inflatable mattresses, to be exact, each of them about a metre from its neighbours. Most of the mattresses were occupied, a dark shape under a grey blanket, but my guide led me to one that was empty, the grey blanket folded neatly ready for me.

"Okay?" she whispered.

"Yes thanks."

She left me to it, her torch dancing its way towards the light at the door.

Once she was gone, I could concentrate on the sound of a sports hall filled with sleeping cyclists. Snoring mostly, at least a dozen voices, a dozen snores all of different tones and volumes and frequencies. I couldn't help myself smiling.

Inside my handlebar bag I now had the items I considered important for sleeping. Sleep was something I had worried about. I am not a good sleeper. Usually I find it difficult to sleep if I especially need to, or if I am worried about what will happen if I don't get enough sleep. The easiest way to sleep, I find, is firstly to be tired, and secondly to want to stay awake to do something important to me at the time. Meetings are good.

My favourite way to get to sleep is to be reading a good book, really keen to find out what happens, and when I get to the stage I'm struggling to keep my eyes open, I put the book down and turn out the light. Mission accomplished. If I fall asleep with the book in my hands and the light on, that's okay too. I'll drop the book and lose my page, and there's the environmental impact of a low wattage bulb being on for a few hours, but I sleep. When I was a child my parents were always turning my light off when they checked on me. MGL does it for me sometimes nowadays.

But it doesn't work, of course, if I need the sleep and I'm worried about not sleeping. If I couldn't sleep well on the way to Edinburgh I would be suffering tomorrow. Worrying about not sleeping would stop me from being able to concentrate on reading. And reading would be antisocial when sharing a bedroom with 200 other people. Instead, and I planned this, my method for the night was to listen to a mp3 meditation track on my phone.

There was some hassle involved here. First I unpacked the silk sheet sleeping bag I brought with the intention of converting a rough blanket into comfortable bedding, then I stripped out of my lycra and wriggled into it, and then in near darkness I had to locate and retrieve my headphones from the handlebar bag, all the while trying not to make rustling noises with an errant plastic bag in there. I had to find my phone from the pocket - one of three - on the back of my LEL2013 jersey. I had to find the headphones that I left on the bed while I searched for the phone. I put the earbuds into my ears, then realised they were the wrong way round and would fall out and I rearranged them. I found the phone again and plugged it in, and, shielding the bright screen under the blanket for fear of disturbing other sleepers, I found the track I needed to play. The Headspace meditation on sleep. I recommend it.

Of course by the time I found it, I needed to find the earbuds again and put them back in my ears, and then hold them in place while I eased myself into a comfortable sleeping position.

I started listening, and the soothing voice was quite relaxing, as it needed to be after the considerable stress involved in setting it up. Sadly, it only lasted a couple of minutes before it stopped, midsentence, and for no apparent reason.

I lay still, wondering if I was relaxed enough to sleep, and if it was worth trying to start the track again. I listened to other people sleeping and to my heart pounding where I was so clearly not relaxed enough to sleep. Laziness has its own inertia, but I did eventually decide to try again.

The second time was more successful. The track wasn't very entertaining, but I woke a long time later since the earbud in my right ear was uncomfortable where I was lying on it. I took it out without being tempted to look at the time and quickly fell back asleep. When I next woke, it was because somebody had taken a firm but gentle grip on my shoulder to rouse me. It was time to get up.

It was almost light, although the hall was in a basement and there was only the slenderest of windows to allow daylight to enter. But it was six o'clock on a July morning, and therefore clearly it was fully daylight outside.

The hall was empty. Where last night the torch beam had shown hundreds of sleeping figures, and there was the sound of snoring from every quarter, now there was a sense of great space and a neat grid of empty mattresses, each with a discarded grey blanket forlornly left behind. There was silence, which added to that sense of space.

And there was guilt. I was instantly guilty of sleeping in. Of being soft. Being lazy. My companions had been on the road for hours. Time was ticking away.

I gathered my thoughts, and then I gathered my few possessions. The clean shorts and shirt which made up my pillow, the wires of my headphones. My phone, beside my knee inside the silk. I dressed, packed, got up, and walked quickly and guiltily across the wooden floor of the Sports Hall and up the stairs into the fluorescent lights of the foyer and dining area upstairs.

Malcolm Dancy

CHAPTER SEVEN
Luck, and How to Live

Actually it was still pretty dim when I set off. Dawn. A word I don't use very often, a part of the day that seems to exist more in theory than in practice. It was cool, but the sky was clear and the wind was firmly behind me, and it was going to be another warm day.

And I was totally alone. For the first time on my journey, I was the only cyclist on the road.

Which meant that there was nobody but me to blame for the navigational responsibilities. Although I had demonstrated something of a lack in that department when I had momentarily been on my own, so far as aiming towards Edinburgh was concerned, taking the first available wrong turning in Cambridgeshire, I would have to make a go of it now.

I couldn't even wait for the next rider to catch up with me. I didn't have the patience for more than a couple of minutes, let alone an hour. The road was empty.

I managed the right out of the school, and the left at the next T junction that took me towards the town centre. Right at traffic lights and straight out of the small town. Then a left turn signposted Walesby, after 0.9km. All very easy. The GPS unit on my handlebars, whilst unable to point out the junctions for me, did allow me to know the distance, so I could watch for the 0.9 km to come up and bring me to 1.6 km total, the first mile of the second day.

The problem was that the route sheet, in the transparent pocket at the top of my handlebar bag, and always turned to the right page, was very difficult to read while I was moving, or at least it was difficult to read safely, due to the size of print and the vibrations of the bike. And I was very reluctant to stop just to read them.

The problems are not in the first mile but after twenty or so, when you have other things on your mind besides the navigation, and you forget yourself until you are well off the route.

I didn't get lost in Walesby. Walesby was a small village marked by a confluence of small lanes; the road twisted around the houses and then the village was behind me.

And I was going uphill. I'd changed gear a few times already, and it was only when I found myself standing on the pedals to keep up my momentum that I took in the full significance of what was happening.

A hill.

After 300km and one day's cycling.

I was out of the Fens.

I felt true joy at this. The change in the landscape marked the beginning of the more exciting terrain. The challenge of mountains was ahead of me. The Fens were interesting in themselves, as a concept, as an example of artificial landscape, but they were boring to cycle through. Hurrah for the hills.

The hill went on. It was about a 10% gradient, and it was a long hill. The summit looked to be just up the road, but every minute I cycled, it still looked to be just up the road. My hill-climbing muscles that had been happy to be included in the adventure once again were now in pain.

But eventually the summit really was at the top of this bit of road, and there was a view, of kinds, a panorama of farmland dipping away in all directions, and a radar station to one side full of purposeful-looking giant white golf ball installations. I stopped pedalling for a moment, content that the bike would roll without immediately slowing to a halt now. I took a deep breath, the cool air absolutely delicious, the way that water is delicious to the thirsty. The sky was brightening, the sun would be up soon, and it was wonderful to be alive.

And so on. You don't get that sort of thing in Flatland. The landscape didn't look exactly mountainous, but a hill is a hill. I noticed the road I was cycling on was called High Street, although it was absolutely a country lane and not, and never had been, a metropolitan thoroughfare. High in altitude rather than importance.

I met another cyclist. At first a dot in the road up ahead, disappearing into the trees at the next slight bend in the road the moment I glimpsed him, so that I wondered if the dot I thought I saw was anything at all. Then I saw him again, and well enough I could be sure it was a person on a bicycle and not some trick of the light. Then as the figure grew larger, I could make out a cycling jersey, and cycle shorts, enough information to determine a cyclist rather than just a person who happened to be riding a bicycle today, at this moment. I considered the odds that a cyclist would be out in the country lanes at six thirty on a weekday morning and be on the same road as the LEL route by coincidence, and came up with something like this:

Number of cyclists in the UK: 3 million according to the CTC

Percentage of cyclists who cycle recreationally as opposed to commuting: 10%

Percentage of adults retired or on holiday in July: 20%

Percentage of cyclists who are out early on a weekday: 2%

Percentage of adults who live within thirty miles of here: 0.01%

Combining all of these numbers in my head gave me about 12% of a cyclist spread out over all the country lanes in the vicinity. Which would be about one leg from mid-thigh downwards. Or an arm.

Nevertheless, as I gradually approached this rider, I was on the lookout for signs, and was happy to see the white card with the name and rider number fixed to a black saddlebag. One of us, for sure. A middle-aged man, which I would have bet on, that being the most common demographic (although fortunately not by a completely overwhelming margin). He was older and slower than me, with a yellow waterproof despite the lack of rain in the air.

"Come far?" I asked him as I pulled alongside.

He looked blank for a moment, taking in that I too was marked as LEL, as well as fitting the middle-aged man description. He smiled, "You could say."

"Did you set out from Market Rasen?"

"Market Rasen, aye."

"What time did you set out?"

"Today? About five thirty."

Only 5 minutes before me. Which disappointed me for a moment - that it had taken me nearly an hour to catch him up, although there's no logical reason for that disappointment. We'd covered less than 20 kilometres, and five minutes was at least a kilometre.

We chatted for a few moments before the difference in our cruising speeds saw me drawing ahead and leaving him, riding alone once more.

The sun rose above the horizon. The landscape became flat again, or at least flattish. Normal flat rather than Fen flat. I passed a couple of other cyclists, enjoying brief chats with each one before moving on. It got warmer, another beautiful day in the making. And I was heading for the Humber Bridge, which I'd never seen before and was something I'd been looking forward to riding over since the route was published. I could smell the sea.

Now was good time to get lost.

I missed a turning and that was it. I was excited by the thought of the bridge and of water, and perhaps subconsciously that is what got me to the water's edge. Or almost. A small roundabout in front of a car park with the bridge as a backdrop, and a dead end beyond the car park. According to Google Maps, and it was a time for Google Maps, I was within spitting distance of the water's edge. Or, more specifically, the Water's Edge Visitor Centre, which has a lot going for it, with a Nature

Reserve, and a sailing club, and views out on the Humber, and of the Humber Bridge itself. What it doesn't have is access to the bridge, from which it is separated by a small brook.

At this point I met my fourth cyclist of the morning. He was also lost.

"Do you have a map?" he asked. He had a soft American accent, and a lovely titanium framed bike with German lights on it (Edelux) and a leather saddlebag.

"Sort of."

We both looked at my phone with its tiny map, and at the route sheet.

"We need to backtrack quite a way," he said.

About a mile, in fact. And as we set off, I could see the cyclist I had passed five minutes back coming towards us, about a half mile distant, passing on a road parallel to ours, and clearly going the right direction.

We went back to the town of Barton upon Humber, and then along the interestingly named Far Ings Road, towards the bridge, and then right under it. There were a couple of of blokes marshalling this point, standing in front of a blue sign that signalled the cyclepath across the bridge.

"This way," one of them said, pointing.

"Right ho."

I didn't realise at the time, but the route sheet didn't say which of the two cyclepaths you should take over the Humber Bridge, and the marshals were there to make sure we didn't take the wrong side, which would have lead to all kinds of consequences I never fully grasped. The path went south for a hundred yards on a slight incline, then turned around to rise up the rest of the way to bridge level, giving me an aerial view of the same two marshals.

The bridge was pretty cool. The path was bumpy, but I had no intention of going fast across it anyway. I love the sense of height and the heightened view you get from a bridge and I stopped to take several poor quality photographs. Having seen exactly four cyclists on the road all day, I was with two of them now on the bridge, and I was shortly overtaken by the gentleman on the Moulton seen in the photograph. Almost busy.

The Moulton gentleman was a young man in his twenties who was called Peter as far as I can remember. He was sharply dressed for a cyclist, in a good fitting jersey and Rapha three quarter length shorts, a natty cap instead of a helmet. His Moulton was a beautiful orange, and he was in a good mood.

"I'm definitely enjoying myself," he said. "The way I see it, this is fantastic value for a holiday."

"I guess so." I hadn't thought of it as a holiday, but of course it was. It wasn't an expedition, now, was it?

"You couldn't have a touring holiday for five days for this price."

This price only possible due to the free services of the hundreds of volunteers. He was right.

"That's why I don't get these guys trying to do it in three days. What's the point?"

To be fair, I *can* see the point in trying to achieve London Edinburgh London in three days, or four days or whatever. But I could certainly see the point of taking your time. We all had a little over 118 hours allocated, and my intention, and obviously Peter's, was to enjoy them all. I'd never really thought about the money, which was a small consideration compared to the time away from family and the sheer hard work involved in making it happen. But now I did think about the money, and it was true. £45 per day for all the food and drink you needed as well as basic accommodation is difficult to beat. I did wonder why somebody who could afford Moulton and Rapha was concerned with value for money over five days cycling, but perhaps it was by minding his money sensibly that he could afford these things.

After the bridge there was a short section through the woods on a cycle path. By the time we reached tarmac again, the small group of riders who had crossed the bridge at the same time as me had dispersed and I would continue to Pocklington on my own.

The weather was still good, the sun was shining and the wind still blew in the right direction. But there was water on the ground, puddles. Clearly it had been raining very recently, just not where I was. There had been storms the night before, there were branches blown off trees. I was being lucky with the weather.

I discussed this with the next cyclist I passed along the road.

The next cyclist along the road was an American gentlemen with a fabulous beard. I could see the beard on either side of his face as I approached him from behind. I got the idea he was American from the beard alone. As I closed in on him, his jersey, advertising long-distance cycling events in California, and his nationality printed on his rider card, confirmed it.

"Good morning!" I said.

"Good morning!"

"We're being lucky with the weather," I said, opening the conversation with our national obsession.

"We certainly are."

"But I suppose we're going to get rained on at some point."

"Oh, *that* is a certainty."

"You look like you had done this sort of thing before," I said.

"I have. This is my sixth long distance ride."

A little while after I left him, I came across a fallen tree that blocked half of the road. I was very glad I wasn't on the road at the same time as the wind that brought it down.

Pocklington is a small market town and civil parish situated at the foot of the Yorkshire Wolds in the East Riding of Yorkshire, England, approximately 13 miles (21 km) east of York. It is commonly referred to as "Pock", or so I was told by one of the volunteers there. The town's skyline is dominated by the 15th-century tower of All Saints church. The town's architecture is a mixture of quaint old houses and modern buildings and there are several unusual street names reflecting its history from the Iron Age onwards. It is now considered to be a commuter town for York, Hull and Leeds, at least by the person who wrote the Wikipedia page. I didn't see much of that. I just followed signs to the control.

Which was at Lyndhurst School, a feeder primary school attached to the independent Pocklington School, the latter being a prestigious institution that counts William Wilberforce and Tom Stoppard amongst its alumni. Not surprisingly, after getting up at five, and having cycled 84 km, the architecture of this venerable educational establishment was lost on me. I followed the temporary plastic signpost in London Edinburgh London colours, the last part of the stage marked out with temporary barriers, and I was there.

The scene reminded me of a disaster area. It was the night after the storm. The small, modern dining hall for 100 or so junior school pupils was transformed. There weren't many people there, Most of them wearing the red T-shirt uniform of the volunteer force together with gaunt, drawn, expressions. Everybody looked tired.

"What was it like here last night," I asked the woman who served me pasta.

She rolled her eyes. "It was crazy," she said, with a middle European accent. She was from Hungary. Her husband had come across to do the ride, and she was here supporting him, and supporting everybody else too.

"We ran out of food, beds, everything. Everybody was here at the same time."

It had been a good decision to stop last night.

I had a bag drop at Pocklington. A pink draw-string cotton bag which contained another pair of cycling shorts, a spare base layer, spare chocolate, dried fruit, more dried fruit, and a spare battery. There were two women the desk where you asked for your bag, and while one of them went to find the one labelled R6, I asked her colleague how things had been overnight, to get a second opinion.

"Crazy," she said.

They had run out of food, having to send people to nearby supermarkets to stock up again. They ran out of sleeping spaces. At the very peak time there was a waiting list for a bed, and a maximum permitted sleep of two hours. At this time I had been soundly asleep 84 km up the road.

"There's even somebody left their shoes behind," the woman said.

"What, cycling shoes?"

"That's right."

"How can you forget your cycling shoes?"

She didn't know. I imagined that somebody had taken the wrong pair of shoes by accident, but it wasn't my problem.

And here we come onto the subject of faff.

I had opted for the early night yesterday, and had clearly slept for longer than is the norm amongst the long distance cycling crowd, and I had ground to catch up. I had arrived in Pock with three hours and 20 minutes in hand, but the idea was that over the first few days I built up a safety margin of time in case of accident or mechanical problem. I wanted more than three hours in the bank.

So the sensible thing would be to have a quick second breakfast, exchange clean clothes from the drawstring bag with dirty ones from my saddlebag, recharge my water bottles, and get on the go again.

That was the sensible thing.

On the other hand, when you have just spent several hours cycling mostly on your own, and suddenly you are in a warm and convivial environment, with tea and pasta and cake and company, it is easy to forget that need for efficiency. This is the danger of faff.

In life I am something of an expert on procrastination. It is therefore no great surprise to anyone that the 15 minute stop is beyond me. Here is what happened:

Monday 29th July 0920; arrived at Pocklington control. Proceed to Control point. Chat to volunteers.

0925; walk into dining area

0929; pick up tray and queue for tea, food, et cetera.

0934; put tray down on empty table, return to bicycle to collect handlebar bag.

0936; drink tea.

0940; collect bag from bag drop area. Talk about previous night.

0945; eat breakfast, while exchanging clothes etc between handlebar bag and drawstring bag.

0955; get another cup of tea.

0959; return drawstring bag to bag drop area.

1001; arrange route sheet in map pockets of handlebar bag.

1004; return tray. Take handlebar bag out to bicycle. Go to toilet and apply Sudocrem.

1009; collect bottles from bike and refill.

1010; sit on bicycle daydreaming for a few moments while eavesdropping fellow cyclists and putting helmet and gloves on.

1015; proceed towards Thirsk, now with 2 1/2 hours in hand.

By this time it was warming up, with the sun shining, and the wind blowing vigourously. The route out of Pocklington took us on small windy country roads, only a single car's width, some of them with grass growing in a line along the middle where the tarmac was missed by car tyres. It was a beautiful day and I was enjoying myself.

There were signposts for Stamford Bridge and I remembered from my school history lessons that Stamford Bridge was the site of the historic battlefield where King Harold defeated a Viking army before heading down to do fatal battle with William at Hastings. But we didn't go to Stamford Bridge, we went through Skirpenbeck and Buttercrambe and Barton le Willows instead, wonderfully named dwelling places, although I don't remember anything about them.

I met Graham here. I had passed a number of people on the road since Pocklington, but none of them stayed with me for any length of time. When I passed Graham, a man in his 60s on a traditional audax bike, I didn't expect him to catch on to my wheel and stay with me, but he did.

After five minutes of sitting behind me, he drew level and I thought I had better engage him in conversation.

"How are you doing?"

"Not so good," he said.

"Oh?"

"It's my own fault. I set out too fast yesterday and I'm paying for it now." He sounded miserable.

"You seem to be doing okay now," I said.

Graham shook his head.

We cycled side by side for a while and then he dropped back as a car overtook us and rode behind me for a couple of miles. The sun rose into the blue sky and it continued to get warmer. It was a beautiful day.

The road came to a crossroads with the main A68 road. We had to cross one carriageway then wait in the space halfway across for a few moments before crossing the rest of the way. The route continued on the other side, and we cycled between golden fields of wheat. It was very nice.

"It doesn't get better than this," I said.

Graham didn't agree. "I'm not enjoying this. I should have trained more."

The road rose gently into the distance in front of us, but the wind was still behind us and it was still a beautiful day for cycling. For a moment I left Graham behind. The road ahead of me twisted and turned as it went up towards a wooded hilltop. I stood on the pedals to reach the top.

There was a statue in front of me atop a large column out in the middle of nowhere. I got off my bike to take some photographs and to wait for Graham to catch me up.

By the time I had taken some photographs, I looked to see where Graham was, and he was still a long way behind me, and I wondered if I should bother to wait for him. From my point of view, his conversation wasn't a benefit, and the selfish thing to do would be to continue.

I did feel a little guilty about it though.

The monument was erected to the seventh Earl of Carlisle, one George Howard, and this was my introduction to the amazing spectacle that is Castle Howard, one of the biggest and most ostentatious of mansions in the country. The main buildings have been used as film settings numerous times, in particular for the TV series and film of *Brideshead Revisited.* But it was the grounds that made an impression today, for their sheer scale as much as anything else: they cover quite a large part of Yorkshire, and are landscaped and decorated with walls and arches and monuments you encounter one by one as you cycle northwards through them.

The road descended in a dead straight line that passed through an arch in what looked like a mediaeval castle wall, though one clearly built much more recently and in much more pristine condition than it would otherwise have been. From there started a long climb towards another arch at the crest of the hill, this second arch running through a building, the gatehouse called The Stray. From here, it was downhill to another monument, The Obelisk, a great column thirty metres tall set inside a small roundabout.

Going straight on here, the route took me on past the lake to take a left hand turn signposted Terrington, which headed us into the wind.

The headwind was of no great consequence, because the road through the Howardian Hills here gave plenty of shelter from it, unlike the situation in the Fens. I continued in good spirits, making decent progress, passing and chatting to a number of other cyclists on my way. I reached the control at Thirsk just after one o'clock.

Thirsk is a small town of about 5000 people centred on a mediaeval market square that boasts a rather lovely clocktower. The town is a local tourist attraction serving as a base for the Yorkshire Dales. The control was at Thirsk School, considered a "thoroughly good school with some outstanding features" by Ofsted.

Just inside the door to the dining area of the school, somebody had made a large poster showing the LEL route, with a map marked out with the roads we had used and would use, and photographs representing each of the control towns. This was the only place I saw the rather lovely clocktower in the mediaeval Market Square. Up to now I had covered 400 km, and seeing this in front of me on a large map was quite impressive. I was more than half way to Edinburgh, and the poster clearly showed that. I went to queue up for lunch filled with optimism.

Alistair was in the dining room halfway through his lunch. I was delighted to join him, and we set to discussing the rather strange meal in front of us, this being a potato pie with roast potatoes and some kind of potato fritter. Very much a variation on a single theme. As a source of pure carbohydrate to replenish energy supplies, however, it could not be faulted, and mugs of tea washed it down nicely.

Alistair was happy to wait for me so we could set off for Barnard Castle together, but since he is even better at faffing than I am, it was me who was happy to wait for him.

CHAPTER EIGHT
Hills

Alistair and I became the nucleus of a small group of cyclists who covered 67km to Barnard Castle more or less together. It was a scenic, hilly ride that didn't go remotely near a town of any size. The roads were damp with recent rain, but it didn't rain on us at all.

We passed Otterington, population 361, and Newby Wiske, population 174, which contains nearby Wiske Hall, a Grade II Listed Building which has been home to the North Yorkshire Police Head Quarters since 1976, then Warlaby, population unknown, at least to Wikipedia, Yafforth, Population 174 (again!) Then Streetlam, whose population fluctuates around 25 but enjoys the company of large numbers of summer tourists walking the Wainwright Coast to Coast route, which passes through the town.

Halfway through this stage, Moulton, population 208, contains Moulton Hall, a 17th-century manor house, owned and maintained by the National Trust. To a cyclist the word Moulton is synonymous with the bicycle designed by Sir Alex Moulton and built at his factory in Bradford on Avon. This is the kind of bike Peter was riding when I met him at the Humber Bridge. Sir Alex Moulton made his name with the wheels and suspension for the original mini, which was designed by his friend Sir Alec Issigonis. It was Moulton's small wheels and rubber suspension that enabled Issigonis to make the mini as small as it was. Moulton applied the same logic to his design of bicycle, aiming to make a machine that was compact enough to be easily stored or carried on public transport in addition to having good acceleration and suspension. Moulton bicycles are famously expensive but have a seriously loyal fan base, occasionally called Moultoneers. The village of Moulton in Yorkshire has nothing whatsoever to do with either designer or bicycle, so far as I know.

The ride continued through the villages of Middleton Tyas, Melsonby and Forcett, populations 630, 735, and 135, after which we met a rider coming the other way who urged us to turn around.

"The road's blocked. You'll not get through that way."

"Why not?"

"There's a tree down. You can't get through Ovington at all."

Our group of riders stopped at the junction signposted Ovington to discuss this news. Our messenger rode on. There was no obvious alternative route, especially not to people equipped with route sheet and/or GPS but without local knowledge or a decent map. But eventually I noticed that the route sheet mentioned Ovington, but the town name was only printed in normal font, as supposed to the **bold font** which signified a place we would actually pass through, so the likelihood was we wouldn't need to meet the fallen tree.

So we carried on and didn't meet a fallen tree. We turned off away from Ovington at Caldwell, population 115, heading due west towards Whorlton, population 205, where we crossed the River Tees on a wonderfully wide but rickety wooden bridge. From there it was 7 km to Barnard Castle, where the control was in Teesdale School.

Shortly before we reached Barnard Castle, we met Chris Lovitt, stationery at the roadside with his black cargo bike. This is a machine with small 24 inch wheels and an elongated wheelbase to accommodate a large luggage platform. Chris is famous for taking a dog with him on rides, the dog sitting in the platform, although on this occasion there was no sign of the dog. I had seen Chris at the start, but I hadn't seen him since.

He was riding such an unsuitable bicycle in an attempt to raise £3000 for the charity Canine Partners, which trains "assistance dogs" to transform the lives of people with disabilities. Considering he was riding a bicycle twice the weight of mine, whose design included something of a windbreak at the front, he was doing all right. Given that he had started several hours after me, he was doing better than I was. Or he had been prior to the failure of his steering.

Because of the large luggage platform, the handlebars needed to be connected to the front forks by a long bar that ran underneath the platform. On inspection, the connection seemed to be secured by a single nut which had worked its way loose and fallen on the road somewhere behind us. When the bar became disconnected, poor Chris had no control whatsoever over the direction his bike would proceed, and he considered himself fortunate that it had proceeded into the verge at the side of the road, and perhaps even more fortunate that this had happened on a quiet section of the route, rather than a busy downhill.

A group of us quickly assembled, all trying to lend a hand. In between all these hands, a new nut was found, and spanners also, I'm proud to say one of them was mine, to fix it in place. It seemed likely that Chris would be able to carry on, although everybody seemed to agree that the design of the steering bar, and particularly its connection, was asking for trouble. Confident that the problem was solved, and that I had done my bit, I continued on my way.

Chris arrived at Barnard Castle only a quarter of an hour after I did, but unfortunately he didn't continue from that point.

There is something very special about hills. Whilst cycling up hill is undeniably hard work, it can be also extraordinarily satisfying.

The philosophy of "no pain, no gain", is a common one in cycling circles. Certainly something that is achieved without a modicum of effort will be less valued than something which has been earned, but I think there's more to it than that.

Perhaps more relevant is the propensity for a hilly section of road to be scenic. This is not pure coincidence, of course. As I learnt in geography lessons thirty-five years ago, areas of the map with lots of contour lines are less likely to contain urban developments and population centres. For reasons unknown to me, certainly on a psychological or biological level, we find peaks and slopes and undeveloped woodland attractive.

A long climb, one where you can see the peak you have to ascend while you are still riding along a flat road, is the best. For here you have continual motivation in the seeing of it, as well as the obvious inclination of the road, the promise of a view to ponder while you get your breath back, and the further prize of a long, exhilarating descent as a reward.

Yad Moss at 888m is the highest point on the 2013 LEL route. A graph of elevation against distance for the stage between Barnard Castle and Brampton (commonly called a route profile) is a long up and then a long down, approximately similar to the normal distribution curve you will meet in studies of statistics. Near the summit is one of the very few ski stations in England, open just a few days a year, and run very much by volunteers, but a ski station nonetheless.

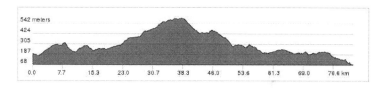

We had to ride the stage that night. To stop so early in the evening would have left us well behind schedule. I was still clinging to the naive assumption that the way to do this thing was to cycle most of each long summer day and stop for a decent and well-earned sleep afterwards. No doubt it is perfectly possible to do a long distance audax like that, only you'd need to be making higher speeds than I was. Most people seemed to succeed on the barest minimum of sleep.

Eating pasta, drinking tea, and loading portable and easy-to-eat snacks like flapjacks into my handlebar bag, I got talking to Richard, who had caught us up just before the control at Barnard

Castle and who was also ready to cycle to Brampton that night. We sent off at about 10:30 p.m.

The road to Brampton is very roughly east to west, and this would be directly into the wind, and for most of it there would be little shelter by way of trees or buildings to take the brunt of it. On the positive side, the stage was ridiculously simple to navigate, being mostly along the one road and requiring only 14 lines on the route sheet. And on the even more positive side, it was a hill to be conquered.

After the usual faff — the filling of water bottle, the emptying of bladders and the application of Sudocrem and the everybody waiting for everybody else — a group of six of us, including Richard and Alistair and obviously myself set off to the best wishes of a handful of red T-shirted sleep-deprived volunteers still on duty at this late hour.

We were in good spirits. Although the moon was shrouded in cloud, there was camaraderie and the ridiculously bright lights of modern LEDs. I like riding at night anyway: it is a different experience. The roads are empty, you can't see very much, but what you can see is different. There's a novelty about it.

The gradient started gently. It was reasonably flat leaving Barnard Castle, and we could make a decent pace and still have breath enough for conversation. Imperceptibly it got steeper, the road put up more resistance, the level of talk diminished, and gaps began to appear between riders. By the time you noticed you were definitely going uphill, the landscape was already more exposed, and the wind was very obvious.

If I have lead you to believe all cyclists enjoy the challenge of a hill climb I am guilty of misleading you. I love hills. But it might be relevant to mention that I weigh 60 kg (that's nine stone to anyone that prefers the weights and measures of a bygone age) when soaking wet. Even when I am at my fittest, I have a body mass index that goes with advice for me to see a doctor because I am apparently underweight. Chris Froome, I believe, has a similar BMI and is a great athlete, so clearly I have great potential as a cyclist and I am not going to worry about my BMI.

Soon enough, I was no longer riding with a group of six riders, I was riding with Richard, and we enjoyed one another's company for the hour or so that we were approaching Yad Moss.

I quickly found out that it was Richard who had lost his shoes at Pocklington.

"So what did you do?"

"One of the volunteers drove me to York. It was the fastest I've ever bought a pair of shoes." Even so it was three hours before Richard was ready to leave, three hours he had lost from his schedule. He had already told his mates to go on without him.

Richard's LEL number began with a C, which meant he had left Loughton three and a quarter hours before me. He was worried about whether or not he would be able to catch up that lost time.

"You're making good progress now," I told him.

"Yeah but I'm feeling tired. I think I'll probably quit at Brampton."

I told him what had happened to his shoes. He had guessed the same. I wondered whether the rider who was now in possession of Richard's shoes had noticed yet.

"I needed some new shoes anyway."

The landscape was changing. Fewer and fewer trees, fields marked out by drystone walls, and sheep to be seen on the hillsides, and the land sloping away from the road on the left down into a valley. There were tall metal poles at regular intervals along the road.

"Do you think," I asked, "these poles for measuring how deep the snow is in winter?"

Richard didn't. "They're for showing where the road is, when there is deep snow. So the snowplough can find it."

"I suppose that would be useful."

I had forgotten about the ski centre.

We then had a lengthy discussion about Britain's policy on nuclear-power, as you do. Richard had a Ph.D. in economics and worked as a civil servant with responsibility for analysis of the energy sector in general and the nuclear industry in particular, while I have a PhD in nuclear physics and once worked as a research scientist at Sellafield. For completeness I will summarise the conversation. It began with our realisation that we each had experience of the subject and from different angles, we agreed that the UK government's enthusiasm for nuclear power in the early years was very much to do with the production of weapons-grade plutonium, we discussed how in the current economic climate it was impossible to finance any new nuclear plant without government subsidy because of the enormous cost of disposing of radioactive waste and decommissioning said plant at the end of its useful life, and we found that neither of us could be sure that nuclear-power wasn't going to be essential for future energy production given the problem of global warming and the necessity to reduce carbon emissions.

Eventually the bulk of Yad Moss loomed out of the darkness.

The conversation about nuclear power couldn't be maintained while we needed all our breath for the fight. As we neared the summit, the land became frighteningly bleak, without sign of a tree, and the wind, with nothing to oppose it, grew stronger. It was hard, damn it! But hard was good. We kept up a good pace, taking turns on the front to keep up our momentum at the cost of conversation. As we got nearer, I think we even increased our pace, such was our enthusiasm.

At the summit it was kind of flat. It wasn't completely clear if we had got to the top yet or not. Somewhat frustratingly, the road wasn't climbing any more, but it wasn't going downhill yet either. And we needed to keep riding hard because of the wind. The poles for snowplough guidance were still marking out lengths of the road, and as we rode past them we were looking carefully to see if there were any clues as to whether it was going upwards or downwards.

"There's plenty of riders with GPS that can tell them when they have reached the top," I said, not very usefully.

"I don't know how we are going to cope without knowing," Richard said. I wasn't sure if he was being sarcastic or not.

Then, out of the gloom, I could see two people standing up by one of the poles. "Is this it? I shouted.

"We think so!" one of them shouted back.

We didn't pause for this conversation, there was still the sense of urgency within us, and the wind was too strong for any comfortable resting place. We rode on.

The road remained flattish for a long time yet, but to me the riders stopped at the side of the road represented the summit, and I stopped worrying about it. A couple of minutes later, the gradient began to tip forwards.

The speed went up. I changed to a higher gear. And again. And again until Richard and I were freewheeling downhill, wind notwithstanding, enjoying the descent we had earned.

A long sweeping descent is always a joy. After grinding your way slowly upwards, the road changing so slowly beneath you, the landscape changing hardly at all, suddenly you are moving. On the descent the road flashes past beneath your wheels, you swing the bike into the bends, you feel the accelerations up through the road and the handlebars and the saddle as you change direction. You feel the surface of the road through the bike. You feel the air rushing past your face. You feel the speed and it makes you feel alive.

The damp dark landscape blurred past, with Richard's back lights dancing red in front of me. He edged away from me, and I hunched down to get as streamlined as I could, focusing intently on the road to take the best line through the curves.

It got cold. I could have predicted that, and added another layer underneath my rainjacket, but having missed that opportunity, I would have to stay cold, because I was enjoying the adrenaline too much to take a break now.

There were lights ahead, two of them. Bicycle lights clearly, red in the mist. Two cyclists, one in front of the other.

We caught them quickly, rolling down the hill significantly faster than they were. And as we drew level, the reason for this became clear. They were not riding bicycles as such, but ElliptiGOs.

The ElliptiGO is something like a cross between a bicycle and a running machine. It was invented by Brian Pate and Brent Teal in 2005. Brian was a marathon runner and triathlete who had damaged his hips and knees through injuries and could only engage in low impact exercise. Finding that cycling took too long to provide a decent workout, he was using an indoor elliptical trainer, but wanted to be outside. Brent was also a triathlete and ultramarathon runner, but also an engineer. Together they worked on combining the elliptical trainer and the bicycle to make the machine that they called the ElliptiGO. And this is how it works: the rider stands on it, wearing running shoes, and moves his legs up and down in the same manner as one might when running, with the crucial difference that the feet do not leave the platforms they are on. Because they still make use of a chain to connect the motion of the platforms to the rotation of the rear wheel, they would still be legal for Paris Brest Paris, which will not permit any "velocipede" not deemed to be a proper bicycle. They are promoted us a tool for runners to get fit on without risking impact damage to their joints. You can hire one to make laps of Richmond Park for the novelty value. Three brave riders, possibly representatives of the company, were attempting LEL 2013 on these machines, and had generated a great deal of publicity and goodwill through their efforts. Here were two of them.

How are you doing? I shouted as I went past. There was no time for any longer conversation. Both of them replied, I think, but their words were lost to the wind.

We descended down to Alston, where the road was cobbled. There were clear warnings about this in the route sheet, so I was expecting them, although I was in the town rather sooner than I thought, and needed to brake severely to bring the speed down to a level safe enough to avoid catastrophe. To negotiate a wet cobbled road that goes downhill and contains sharp corners as it goes into the centre of the town requires a very slow speed. Slow enough it was no effort to stop when we came to the water feature in the centre of Alston.

Sitting on the low wall that surrounded it was Trickedem, or Tim Decker, eating a Mars bar. The Trickedem was the label on his saddlebag, a yacf alias, and the Tim bit was on his LEL rider label. One is an anagram of the other. He invited us to share his wall. Richard went into the adjacent corner shop to buy something to nibble on and I raided my handlebar bag. We shared our experiences of the ride over the summit, and then we talked about the ElliptiGO boys. Tim had passed them on the way up.

"They look hard work," I said.

"Doing well though," said Tim.

"I thought they would be harder to control with the rider standing up."

Richard said, "Most of the weight of the bike is low down."

"But most of the weight is the rider, not the bike."

I figured that going downhill, the ElliptiGO would be most disadvantaged, with the rider standing up into the wind, the least aerodynamic position possible.

At that point they arrived. We cheered them. At ten o'clock on a wet Monday night, this noise may not have been completely welcome to the residents of the town.

"How is it going?"

"Pretty good! It's a great descent."

They didn't hang around though, and continued downhill through the town and away. We continued to enjoy the snacks for another 10 minutes before we got going again. The road was mostly downhill, albeit with one unexpected and painful climb, before we came to Brampton and the control.

CHAPTER NINE
Scotland

The control at Brampton was in the William Howard School, A very large co-educational comprehensive school, which hosted *Brampton Live* every summer for 15 years from 1995 to 2010, a music festival which at one time or another included the Levellers, the Waterboys, Egudo Embako, Richard Thompson, Suzanne Vega, Loudon Wainwright III, Altan, Tommy Emmanuel, and The Bills. It is also linked with a school in Tanzania.

None of this was apparent to me at 11 o'clock that evening, but I was very grateful for tea and something to eat. Tim went quickly to bed,

I had a bag to pick up, so after the first cup of tea I went to collect it, and came back to the dining area for subsequent teas while looking through it. Richard told me he had already quit.

"That's a shame," I said. "I'm sure you would have made it."

"I know what tonight took out of me," he said with finality.

When Alistair arrived, we briefly shared our experiences of the climb, and then I excused myself and went to find a bed, taking my helmet and shoes with me.

I had a quick shower first, and enjoyed hot water, and space in the communal showers appropriate to a whole rugby team all to myself. The sleeping arrangements were as they were in Market Rasen, the same grid of air mattresses in a darkened sports hall to be negotiated by torch light.

To my mind, there was more of a smell to the hall this time and a near continuous racket of farts and snores. Not that I was particularly fussy after spending all day today and all day yesterday in the saddle. I didn't bother with finding the meditation MP3 and the earphones to go with it, but I did get out my sheet sleeping bag. I had asked for a 4 a.m. wake up, feeling that this morning's 5 a.m. start had been overindulgence.

Fully intending to do better with respect to faffing, I managed to drink two mugs of tea and eat a piled-up bowl of muesli and be out on the bike not long after 4:30. This included taking my green Brampton bag drop bag back to the bag drop desk, having jettisoned more dirty clothes and my bike lock and my silk sleeping bag since I was intending to be back at Brampton that night, 300 km and a long day's cycling later. I felt I'd achieved something already as I set off on a promising day, with picturesquely low hanging mist. There was a little bit of pain in my legs, and I was slightly sore in the undercarriage, but I didn't think it was going to spoil my day. And I was cycling to Scotland! It felt good just to think that.

I caught Drew Buck, the man in costume riding the antique French bicycle, after a few kilometres. By that time I'd heard enough people talking about him to know who he was. The bike was something I'd admired the previous day when I saw it parked outside a control; just one look of it gave you the idea it was a serious weight - it was certainly solid enough to last the best part of a hundred years, and it was adorned with a magnificent and enormous front lamp as well as a bunch of plastic grapes. The most interesting thing about the bike was that the lower of its two gears was engaged by pedalling backwards.

"A lot of people, when they see it, they think they're going mad," he told me.

I rode with him long enough for him to have the opportunity to show me - as the road went upwards for a stretch, he stopped peddling, then reversed the action. The bike kept moving forwards.

"I can understand people thinking they're going mad," I agreed. Even knowing he was going to peddle backwards my brain was struggling to take in what I was seeing. Given that this was about six o'clock in the morning, and that I generally get more sleep than I had been recently, it would have been very easy to think there was a malfunction with my thought processes.

I chatted with him for a few minutes, all of this at his cruising speed of about 18km/h, and then pushed on.

I caught Alistair shortly afterwards, and we cycled together to the border, where I felt the need to stop and get photographs. He took a picture of me on my phone, and *vice versa*. Here it is:

I assure you, this is what I look like when I am happy.

Shortly after this we cycled into Gretna Green, a town I have always associated with runaway weddings.

The point of getting married at Gretna Green was that in the 18th Century you could do it in Scotland at the age of 14 as a boy and 12 as a girl, with or without your parents permission, whereas in England you needed to be older and have the permission of your parents. When a toll road was built in the 1770s, Greta Green was the nearest and most accessible town in Scotland, and soon became a Mecca for young couples wanting to marry, if you don't mind a metaphor that mixes religious pilgrimage and eloping teenagers. In 1929, Scottish law raised the age at which a couple could marry to 16, as it is today, but parental permission is still unnecessary, unlike in the rest of the UK.

In Scottish law, if a declaration was made with two witnesses, just about anybody could conduct the marriage ceremony, and it famously fell to the local blacksmith to do the job. Gretna blacksmiths became known as anvil priests, with one of them, a Richard Rennison, performing 5147 marriages. Today, because of the law, and presumably because of the romantic associations of the place, Gretna Green is one of the world's most popular wedding destinations, with 5000 weddings taking place there every year. To put this in perspective, there are only about 30,000 weddings per year in the whole of Scotland.

We passed a number of places where you could get married, most of them with a blacksmith theme, but since Alistair and I were both already married to other people, we cycled through without stopping.

The sun came out mid-morning, and the day quickly warmed up. To celebrate, Scotland wheeled out some of its very impressive scenery. The road ran more or less alongside the A74M motorway, but far enough away that you didn't have to notice it. The sky was blue, with wisps of white cloud. The land was green with the grass and rugged with the geography of the place. I overheard an Italian cyclist describing the landscape as *epic*.

We came to Lockerbie. When I went to university at the tender age of 18, choosing, in my youthful spirit of adventure, St Andrews, a university almost as far away as was possible within the confines of the country, I frequently took trains between my home town of Didcot, a forgettable commuter town in South Oxfordshire, and Leuchars in Fife, the nearest railway station to St Andrews. Such trains at that time were for both Glasgow and Edinburgh, the Edinburgh section then going on to Dundee and perhaps places further north. Since it was uneconomic for any train to go to Edinburgh via Glasgow, in addition to being ridiculously inconvenient for Edinburgh passengers, such trains would physically split into two, and they would do so at Lockerbie. So for a period of four years, while I was in pursuit of my university education, I would come to Lockerbie at the beginning and end of every holiday, spending 15 minutes in railway sidings each time, often in the small hours of the morning, and never once seeing the place.

Of course Lockerbie became more famous when, on 21 December 1988, the American passenger plane Pan Am 103 crashed there following a bomb explosion on board. All 259 people on the plane were killed, and so were 11 people from the town in Sherwood Crescent where the plane's wings and fuel tanks landed, causing a huge explosion and leaving a great crater in the ground. In 2001, a Libyan intelligence officer, Abdelbaset al-Megrahi, was extradited to Scotland and imprisoned for the crime, although the evidence that convicted him appears seriously dubious. The Libyan leader Colonel Gaddafi accepted responsibility for the bombing in 2003 and paid some compensation to families of the victims although he claimed not to have given the order for the attack. More recently there has been speculation that Libya had no involvement in the bombing at all. al-Megrahi died in 2012.

With these two different and strange perceptions of Lockerbie, both of them somewhat abstract, and one of them grotesque, it was nice to see for the first time this pretty little town for its reality, and to do so on a sunny day in July.

The route took us onto the control at Moffat, a pretty little town surrounded by hills, which was once a tourist attraction on account of the spa there, and is now a tourist attraction again, particularly with walkers, on account of the hills around it. Moffatt's heyday was at the end of the 19th century with luxurious hotels springing up to accommodate the numbers of tourists who came to take the waters. As the habit of drinking or bathing in sulphurous waters became less popular, the hotel reinvented itself to cater for the walkers.

A Virgin Discovers Long Distance Cycling

We arrived just before 9 o'clock in the morning, finding our way through a familiar route marked out across the car park of a school. Moffat Academy educates children from nursery all the way up to sixth form, and it traces its history to the local grammar school founded in 1639 by Dr Johnstone. The dining room that was used for LEL was small, intimate, and charming, and I remember while queueing up for the necessary first mug of tea thinking it a shame for such a nice location to only feature once on this five-day adventure; the stage to Moffat represented the beginning of a 200 km loop going up to Edinburgh and then back down to Brampton via Traquair and Eskdalemuir.

With my tea I took porridge. I was encouraged to take porridge; the lovely woman volunteer behind the counter was telling all and sundry in her bright voice that porridge was good for you, and it was lovely, and that now we were in Scotland we should eat it.

So tea and porridge and a flapjack or two and a piece of toast and then more tea and then a keenness to get on with it. It seemed that Edinburgh was very close. It was a beautiful day.

It had indeed shaped up to be a glorious day, but despite the sheer joy of cycling, and the momentum we had built up, and the sense of achievement I knew that I would have on reaching Edinburgh, still I found it impossible to do all the things I needed to do at the control in less than 35 minutes, so it was gone 9:30 when Alistair and I cycled out of Moffat.

The A701 climbed fairly steeply once we were out of the town, and Alistair soon fell behind. The road was busy with cyclists at this time but I didn't find anybody both fast enough and slow enough to match my speed so that I could remain with them for any length of conversation. We ascended quickly into the prime walking territory that kept the hotels in business, climbing from just under 100 m to over 400 m in elevation over about 10 km, leading up to the famous landmark, the Devil's Beeftub.

This dramatic hollow in the hills, 150 m deep, is so named because the Border Reivers, a band of thieves along the Anglo

Scottish border in the time of the Stuart kings of Scotland and the Tudors of England, and who stole from Scots and English alike, and who were known as Devils by those they stole from, were reported to use the place to store their stolen cattle. The novelist Walter Scott wrote of the place that

It looks as if four hills were laying their heads together, to shut out daylight from the dark hollow space between them. A damned deep, black, blackguard-looking abyss of a hole it is.

At the time I was cycling past, none of this local history was known to me, but the sight of it was awesome enough.

The landscape remained spectacular, and the roads challenging in their climbs and and thrilling in their descents. Between the town of Moffat and the outskirts of Edinburgh there was almost nothing by way of a population centre and only three or four key junctions to navigate. The route sheet for the stage was only half the page. And it was heaven for a cyclist.

And all too quickly, it seemed, I was cycling towards Edinburgh city centre.

I have been known to be pedantic. One of the reasons I chose to ride the prologue was because I felt that a ride entitled London Edinburgh London ought to begin in London, rather than Loughton, for example. For the same reason, I felt the mid-point ought to be in Edinburgh, perhaps in front of the Scott Monument on Princes Street. After cycling more than 700 km I was less pedantic. The control was in Gracemount, a suburb in the south of Edinburgh, technically within the city council boundary, at Gracemount High School.

As schools go, Gracemount High is not particularly special, at least not to the casual observer who is preoccupied with other matters and visits on a day in July when it is empty of pupils. To this casual observer it seemed like a generic, modern, concrete-built comprehensive school that had been turned into an LEL stage control by the familiar lane of temporary barriers bearing the familiar red and white banners.

My uncle was standing outside the entrance in a pair of his trademark short shorts and a volunteer red T-shirt, greeting riders and pointing the way in for those who were unable to work it out for themselves.

I stopped and said hello, and allowed him to congratulate me.

"I better let you get some food then," he said.

"They've got you working I see," I said.

"Yes."

He was on his own on entrance duty, but I thought naively that he would probably be relieved by somebody in the next few minutes and he would be able to join me for a chat. I went inside, logged my arrival at 1324, took off my shoes and laid them down carefully somewhere I would remember them, leaving my helmet and sunglasses so that they would not look like somebody else's shoes, and went to get my food and mug of tea.

I took my time, looking up now and again to see if my uncle was coming to join me. I felt a huge sense of achievement, and a regret I didn't have anyone present to share it with for the moment. I phoned Wendy, and had a quick chat to her, and to Junior. Junior was too busy with a computer game to be interested in talking to me even if I had just cycled all the way to Edinburgh. I phoned my mother, only to find that she already knew, since my uncle had called her minutes before.

Presently Alistair arrived and joined me for lunch. When we'd both done eating, he went outside to speak to a bike mechanic and I went with him. While there, I saw there was another bike mechanic volunteer currently unoccupied, and I asked him if he could do something about the creaking noises coming from my gears and bottom bracket that had been annoying me over the last three days. I had already noticed he had a huge bag of very expensive large Campagnolo spanners. 10 minutes later my bike no longer made annoying noises, and Alistair's was receiving a new brake cable where his recent crash had split the old one.

I went back out to the entrance to talk to my uncle. He was stuck there because there were no volunteers to take his place.

"Well," he said, "it's been nice to talk to you!"

"Don't worry, I'm not going yet," I said. I lent my bike up against the fence and sat down on the pavement next to where he was stationed.

Sitting in the sun, I took out some suncream and applied it to my face and arms while we chatted. My uncle had been on duty continuously from about Monday (i.e. yesterday) lunchtime, except for a few occasions where he caught an hour or so's sleep. I learnt that this was not particularly unusual amongst the volunteers, and that volunteering was as much an endurance effort as actually riding the event. While we were talking, some of the last hundred riders were arriving at Edinburgh. It was something of a surprise to me to learn that I was right among the backmarkers for the event. The first rider had arrived on Monday late in the morning, and he had been a whole hour ahead of the second rider. We chatted about my policy of taking my time, enjoying the event, which was not the way he would approach it. I was surprised to hear him say that he couldn't imagine doing a five-day long distance event because he wouldn't be able to sleep.

"In the 24," he said, meaning the Mersey Roads 24-hour time trial, "I catch 10 minutes or half an hour here and there."

"What about the 600?"

"A 600 is about the longest I can do."

"You don't sleep in a 600?"

"No. It's the same as the 24."

We talked about the different types of people that were riding the event, and the different types of bicycles they rode.

While we talked, as if to emphasise the kind of eccentrics we were talking about, Drew Buck arrived. His white trousers were now considerably more dirty than they had been two and a half days earlier, but his smile was still evident.

It was nice, sitting in the sunshine, shooting the breeze. It was nice hearing my uncle talk about the event from the point of view of the volunteers, a point of view that was also tired from lack of sleep, and which also had a sense of achievement and a sense of being part of something on an impressive scale. The big difference was one of giving and taking - my uncle and the hundreds of other volunteers were giving their time and their energy and we riders were accepting their generosity. (I should note that I have in fact accepted my uncle's generosity on numerous occasions.)

For him the event was coming to a close. In a couple of hours there would be very few riders still approaching Edinburgh, and this control would start to shutdown. It took a surprisingly long time for me to really appreciate that it was still only halfway through my event.

"You've lost a good two hours here," my uncle had been telling me.

I assured him I had allowed for that.

Rest can be a dangerous thing. If you don't rest, clearly at some point your body is just going to say no, and grind to a halt. But if you rest for too long, your body gets used to resting, and there's a huge resistance that builds up against any possibility of getting going again. By the time I had spent two hours in Grace Mont High School, all the momentum I had built up in what had been a wonderful day's cycling had dissipated.

So when I started moving, it was with some reluctance. It had already occurred to me the irony of applying suncream in preparation for this next stage, when the reality was now that I had actually started, it was late enough in the day that I didn't really need it. Soon I would need more than just shorts and a short-sleeved jersey to keep me warm.

Alistair had left half an hour earlier, delayed because he looked for me around the control, sure that I wouldn't have left without him. I hadn't, of course, except in the technical sense that I had taken my bicycle and all my belongings and gone to the exit even if I hadn't gone any further than that.

The road to Traquair is another beautiful one, beginning with the gentle ascent away from Edinburgh's suburbs and towards the rolling countryside. Unfortunately with that countryside came cloudy then misty then rainy weather, accompanied by cold, accompanied by something of a sense of fatigue, and quite definitely accompanied by a sense of regret that I sat around in the sun for so long.

I began to feel miserable. I was miserable for a while, long enough to notice that I was miserable and to try reminding myself that I was cycling through a stunning landscape. That seemed to help, although not by any large amount. I could appreciate objectively the stunningness of the landscape, even in the rain, and could appreciate that even in the rain I would normally enjoy this. I could even appreciate the irony that I wasn't appreciating it.

Eventually miserable became less miserable, and the fact that other riders I met were moaning about the weather, and I could moan about the weather to them, seemed to help a little bit. At least I could appreciate that riding in a flat, mundane area with heavy traffic in this rain would be significantly more miserable.

As the road climbed higher, the rain was more intense, but there was a sense of satisfaction in gaining altitude, and everything became so bleak that you had to admire it.

It was a very short stage to Traquair, only 42 km, and that worked for me. I arrived cold and tired at just after six in the evening.

Alistair was leaving as I arrived. He looked a lot fresher than I felt, and was smiling despite the fact he was heading out into the rain.

"Catch you later!" I told him without feeling very convincing.

Traquair is something of a legend already within the 25 year history of the event, a fact I was unaware of at the time. The checkpoint was the village hall, rather than a school, and it was nominated as the checkpoint rather than a control to signify a lack of sleeping facilities there.

The village hall was small and intimate compared to the large modern school reception and dining areas I was getting used to. It was finished in dark wood and had a homely feel to it, to which the smell of wet cyclists made a contribution. The volunteers were cheery and friendly, as everywhere else, but here they were aided with some magnificent specially-commissioned cakes and wee drams of whisky to go with the porridge.

Alcohol and physical exertion do not really go together. More so when you are feeling wretched and still have hours of physical exertion in front of you. On the other hand...

I find it very difficult to refuse whisky. In fact I have had to go and pour myself a wee dram while writing this. And I recognised at the time that what I really needed was a pick-me-up. Even the *idea* of being served whisky was helping to cheer me up.

I was feeling better. While drinking tea and whisky and eating porridge followed by cake, I was pretty much oblivious to everything else, but afterwards I noticed one or two cyclists obviously shivering and being wrapped up in blankets by volunteers. It may be realise how hard all this was, which made me feel better about finding it hard.

I set off within the half hour for Eskdalemuir.

The stage from Traquair to Eskdalemuir was another short one, in fact, officially, this was part B of the first stage going south, and it was only 46 km. The route sheet for it was only five lines long, since those 46 km covered open country with few roads to get lost on. But that is not to say that these 46 km were not hard. It was hilly country, and towards the end of this long day, it was brutal.

And it was also beautiful. After an hour or so, the rain had stopped, and the sun came out, the evening light illuminating the folds of the landscape and producing such a rainbow over the hills to the east that you had to stop cycling for a few minutes just to look at it. I took a photo, but you needed more skill and patience than I have to do it justice.

I met Uryah from Toronto while I was admiring the rainbow.

"Beautiful isn't it?" he said.

"Isn't it?" I agreed. Not the most intellectual of conversation beginnings, but what can you do?

"How you doing?" he asked

"I'm feeling it," I admitted.

"Hard ride," he said.

I smiled, and we set off together, riding south.

Uryah was a young man as LEL riders go, meaning younger than me, perhaps early 30s, with dreadlocks and an elegantly sculpted beard. He was good company. Talking to people who have travelled a long way to participate in this event somehow made it feel more worthwhile to me. Not everybody could get up early and cycle to the start from their home.

The rain came again, and stopped again. The sun remained where it was, shining on us, the rain and the sun coming from different directions so you could have them both at the same time. The rain wasn't very hard, and I didn't mind it at all, as long as the sun was shining, because this was a very beautiful place to cycle.

The rain was no surprise at all, because for a long time I'd known that Eskdalemuir was the wettest place in England. Of course, the fact that Eskdalemuir is actually in Scotland is some indication as to how reliable my knowledge can be. On checking my facts, however, there is at least some truth in my long-held opinion.

There is a weather station Eskdalemuir, part of an observatory built there in 1904 with geomagnetic instruments relocated from Kew Gardens Observatory. The observatory collects data on climate, atmospheric pollution, solar radiation, geomagnetic fields and seismology. The seismic meters at the site recorded the crash of the plane on Lockerbie, 10 miles to the south-west, which made a local earthquake registering 1.6 on the Richter scale. A new array there can detect the seismic signature of nuclear explosions and is part of the international monitoring for the Comprehensive Test Ban Treaty. The weather station there has more than 100 years of data, which confirms a reputation for being wet. And Eskdalemuir does hold the UK record for the wettest half-hour, with 18 mm of rain falling in that space of time on 26 June 1953. The station celebrated its wettest year on record in 2011 when the previous LEL was almost washed out.

Eskdalemuir is a small village, made more famous by frequent mentions on weather forecasts, but it has another claim to fame I had been completely unaware of, one I couldn't fail to notice as we approached the control, because there, behind the trees, was a bloody great temple.

A Tibetan Buddhist temple can give you quite a surprise if it creeps up on you unsuspected. But the Kagyu Samyé Ling Monastery and Tibetan Centre is the largest Buddhist centre in Europe, as well as apparently the 10th most visited tourist destination in Scotland. The centre was set up in 1965 in a former hunting lodge, and has expanded since, and is well established in the local community. In the late 1960s David Bowie and Leonard Cohen were both students, with Bowie later saying that he almost became a monk there.

Approaching the control, Uryah and I were riding in a group of half a dozen riders, happy to be arriving in the last of the evening sunshine. The temple complex on the left had an amusing surreal charm, as did the sight of three barefooted monks walking along the road towards us in a line like gun fighters in an old cowboy movie, only with smiles on their faces instead of grim determination. We waved to them, they waved to us, and then a kilometre up the road was the Eskdalemuir Community Hub where the control had been set up.

The Community Hub used to be the primary school in Eskdalemuir, but when it was closed a group of local people got together to try and make something positive of the loss of a local facility. Despite having both an observatory and a Buddhist temple, Eskdalemuir has no pub, shop or post office, and the idea was to set up a "green" multipurpose building that can be café, shop, meeting rooms and spaces for local enterprises and charities, with the aim, according to their Facebook page, of making Eskdalemuir and its surrounding area an even better place to live. I was so happy to arrive there, so tired, and so hungry, I just assumed it was another school being used for the control. Now I know better, I wish the Community Hub every success.

Alistair was there, halfway through his evening meal, sitting with a big blond-haired German-looking German gentleman called Mario, who spoke excellent English. They had been riding together for much of the day. I sat down with them.

CHAPTER TEN
Down and Up

I had arrived in Eskdalemuir at a 9:15 in the evening, with the Scottish summer sun still in the sky, but it was soon dark. It had been a very long day, and I was ready to rest, but there were no beds in Eskdalemuir for one thing, and for another, once again I couldn't afford the time.

I'd agreed with Uryah that we would set out for Brampton together. I thought it would be faster to cycle with him than with Alistair. Entirely wrongly, as it happens.

We didn't move anywhere until 10. It wasn't so much question of faff, as the need to eat, the need to drink tea, the need to rest, and above all the need to build up the necessary enthusiasm. And in fact, when we did move it was as a reasonably large bunch, maybe as many as a dozen riders.

This 58 km stage was not quite as hilly as the two preceding it, but the steepest climb was in the first 5 km. I felt good at this stage, and Uryah and I quickly left the rest of the bunch behind us.

The route sheet was simple, less than half a page, with the first 20 km on one road, and most of the next 20 km following the A7, then the *Welcome to England* sign and the last 20 km along the A6071 into Brampton. I was content to be getting there and looking forward to going to bed. What could go wrong?

It began to rain. There was no surprise or problem with that, and I was already wearing my yellow Gore-Tex, but this time the water seemed to get into the electronics of my GPS unit, causing it to fail to register any speed at all. I didn't need to know how fast I was going, but up to then it had been very useful to know what distance I had covered; this information, in conjunction with the route sheet, was what I was using to navigate. This was only a minor inconvenience, of course. I wasn't on my own, I was cycling with Uryah, and he was navigating as well. His GPS didn't work either, but surely between ourselves we could work out where we were and which way to go.

My front mudguard was rubbing on the front wheel. This had been happening for the last 750 km, on and off, but now, cycling in the dark, cycling in the miserable rain, frustrated by the sudden failure of the GPS, this was all the more irritating, especially because in the dark I couldn't see what I was doing to push the mudguard out of the way of the wheel. I hurt myself a couple of times touching the wheel with my fingers before I worked out a way of feeling my way along the bicycle forks to reach the connection with the mudguard, but even with this method I couldn't reliably move it to the right position. And anyway, it would drift back again to rub the wheel. So I rode with the wheel rubbing, and the irritating noise it produced, and started to worry that the rubbing might wear a hole in the tyre, leaving me with a catastrophic puncture.

At 9.6 km the route sheet gave warning of poor road surface. In fact it was more precise than that: the poor road surface was from West Kirk bridge at 9.6 km all the way to Bent Path at 19.6 km, rather than a short patch of rough surface at 9.6 km. In retrospect this is a crucial difference. The poor road surface duly arrived, with an outbreak of potholes the full width of the road, difficult to see in the darkness, especially when they were full of water. We were straining our eyes to see them even with the expensively powerful dynamo lights that the average audax rider uses. After a few hundred yards of very uncomfortable riding, there was a yellow triangular road sign warning of poor road surface. Very helpful.

We continued riding. The road was poor, it was raining, I was irritated with my GPS unit and my mudguard, the good feeling that had carried me through the first climb of the stage had gone, and I had remembered how tired I was. Uryah seemed to be happy enough, however, and I was beginning to struggle to keep up with him.

The first turning would be at 21.9 km. I was very much looking forward to this milestone which would show that a third of the stage was done. As time went on I was more and more keenly anticipating this junction, a right-hand turn signposted Lang Holm. And then as time went on and the turning didn't appear I began to wonder if we had missed it. Didn't I remember we gone left at a junction?

Writing this, with the route sheet and with a map in front of me, it's perfectly obvious that there was nowhere we could have gone wrong. We were riding on the A7 and there were no turnoffs before the one we needed.

We passed another temporary yellow triangle marked with the words

WARNING POOR ROAD SURFACE

Or to my mind we passed the same temporary yellow triangle marked with the same words, thus proving that we'd cycled in a loop, repeating at least 10 km a second time. I felt despondent. Worst of all, Uryah, who had hitherto seemed an intelligent young man, was entirely blind to our navigational failure.

"We've gone wrong," I told him, more than once.

"I don't think so," he maintained.

I was cycling much more slowly now. I was tired, I can't say that enough, but now I was demotivated. We were cycling around in circles, in the dark. This was a nightmare.

Other riders caught us. We continued riding through the potholes.

Finally we came to a junction. People said we went right here, and began to cycle off into the darkness.

"Wait!" I shouted. I wanted to be sure. We'd already got lost once.

I couldn't see the route sheet in the dark; the only lights I had were fixed on my bike and could not be easily directed to shine on the my handlebar bag where said route sheet resided. Fortunately there was a light illuminating the T junction sign. I manoeuvred my bike over to it and read: Lang Holm, right at T.

"Yes, it is right," I conceded. The others set off riding, and I followed.

I was hanging on the other back of a group of four or five riders. Uryah was ahead of me. I wanted to catch him up, explain to him where we gone wrong, take the time to get this sorted out properly, but didn't have the legs to catch him up in the first place.

Time passed. Eventually there was a road off to the left. People ahead of me hesitated, then took that road. I stopped again, wanting to check, and one or two riders stopped with me. Left it was. We continued.

I was drifting off the back of this group when Alistair and Mario caught me up.

"What are you doing here?" Alistair asked me.

"Dying," I replied.

"Where is the guy you were riding with?"

"Ahead somewhere," I said.

I was stopping at every junction, insisting quite vocally that we take no chances with directions.

"It is this way," Alistair would be assuring me.

"I want to be sure."

"You're not yourself," he told me, gently.

"That's probably true."

At one point, where there was some traffic at a junction, and the front riders had to wait, we all grouped up again. For a few minutes I found myself riding alongside Uryah again. A little later, he told me he felt really good, and he was going to ride a little bit faster. He pulled ahead and disappeared into the night.

When we passed the *Welcome to England* sign I hardly noticed it. We cycled through a couple of towns much larger than the villages we had passed since the control at Traquair, but I barely registered them. I was on autopilot; I barely registered anything.

But eventually there was Brampton, and I followed other people to the control at William Howard School, and followed them into the bike parking area. I took my handlebar bag and some clothes from my saddlebag and went inside.

I don't remember very much about how I got to bed that night. It was 1:30 in the morning before we arrived, and I must drunk some tea and perhaps eaten something before I went to find my bed. I must have retrieved my bag drop, because it was there beside me when I woke up the following morning. And I must have managed a shower before I went to bed, and dressed in clean lycra for pyjamas, since this is what I woke up wearing, and all of this must have taken some effort of will power. I think Alistair told me that he was going to get up at 4 a.m. to continue, and I think I told him I would need a lot more sleep than that. I don't believe he tried to persuade me differently.

I woke up in pain. Very often, for example after a heavy night's drinking, you wake up and you feel all right until you start moving. The hangover doesn't kick in for half an hour. It wasn't like that today. On the morning of the fourth day, the pain was kicking in as soon as I was awake to notice it.

I thought, *this is what it feels like when you can't go on.* I had the very clear realisation that I might have to quit, and that realisation helped me in a way. To be honest I think I was curious to see just how painful things were. If I couldn't go on I was ready to accept it, I told myself I would just get up and get my things together, and have some breakfast, and see how things were.

I must have stiffened in the night, because moving my muscles really increased the intensity of the pain. Interesting. Once I was sat up on the mattress, I gathered my things into the green Brampton drop bag and into my handlebar bag without moving my legs any more than was necessary. When I stood up, that hurt, but as I walked across the empty sports hall, the pain didn't get any worse, and by the time I reached the exit it was actually receding.

I went to find breakfast. We were out of Scotland and there was no more porridge, but there was muesli, and I poured myself an unfeasibly large bowlful and sat down in front of it. I ate slowly, and drank tea slowly, and took stock of the situation.

It was 7:30 in the morning and cyclists were very much thin on the ground in this school dining area. Most people were clearly on the road already.

By the time I finished my breakfast it was apparent I was going to try to continue. I felt significantly better than I had half an hour earlier, and although my legs ached savagely as I sorted my gear out, and even more when I actually got onto the bike, I was surprised to find I could bear it.

For the first time now, I was retracing my pedal revolutions, cycling south on the same roads I had cycled north on. And that meant climbing Yad Moss again.

I was cycling in the opposite direction, and the wind was the same as it had been two days previously, so it was behind me now. And I was cycling on a sunny morning rather than a damp evening, the hills were inspiring in the early light, and the day was getting warmer. My legs hurt less now I was cycling, as if the pain was giving up now it realised it had failed to stop me.

I can honestly say I found it easier riding over Yad Moss the second time than I did extracting myself from my bed that morning. Back on the bike, there was no doubt that I would continue and that I would finish. I was enjoying myself again.

Alston, at 30 km into the ride, was more attractive in the light than it had been in the dark, but it was now too early for the nice café to be open in the morning instead of it being too late for it to be open in the evening. The steep, cobbled road, now uphill, I managed to negotiate by finding a route along the deserted pavement where it was smoother. From there, climbing up to the summit, I passed a handful of other cyclists, all of them alone or in groups of two, and to each of them I bade good morning and made some kind of favourable comment about the weather.

Passing the summit, it was still difficult to tell exactly which part of the road was the highest, but riding with a tail wind there was less need to have that psychological marker. Cycling down the hill with the wind behind me, using my biggest gear, glancing every now and again at the speed on my bicycle computer, I kidded myself I was making up for lost time. The speed felt good.

Coming into Barnard Castle, I noticed the huge 12th Century castle the town is named after, something I had somehow failed to notice coming the other way. I arrived at the control with a healthy appetite for a second breakfast.

Much to my surprise, I met Alistair and Mario at the control, as they were finishing their own second breakfast.

"Good to see you alive," Alistair said.

"Good to *be* alive," I said.

We had a chat about what a great day for cycling it was, about sleep deprivation, and about what an idiot I had been the night before. I said how good it was to have people to look out for me while I was being such an idiot.

Alistair outlined his new plan: less faff. He was inspired by Drew Buck, the man on the antique French bicycle in the beret and striped Breton shirt. Drew was doing well if he could manage 20km/h on that bike, but he kept his average speed up by spending little time at the controls. I don't think he got very much sleep either. Alistair thought that by spending less time sitting and chatting as well are spending less time sorting out bottles and Sudacrem, it would be much easier to arrive within the time limits.

Therefore we set off relatively briskly. It was good to have companionship on the road again, catching up with Alistair's morning ride, and getting to know Mario, the giant German of Italian descent who was full of good humour.

At Woolton, the route sheet instructed:

Descend! Hairpin bend! To cross River Tees! Wooden bridge!

Descending onto the bridge early on the stage rather than right at the end gave us more opportunity to appreciate the iron suspension bridge erected in 1831, with its beautiful setting and the graceful arch of the suspension cables, and the copious signage warning of the narrow road and the weak bridge, and the illegality of overtaking there. Despite the description on the route sheet, I couldn't see any trace of wood in the structure.

The route profile of this stage is mostly downhill, although there were plenty of short uphill sections to make it a hard ride. But it was sunny, and generally there was enough shelter from the crosswind for it to be easy riding.

To give you an idea of the things that are important in the generally under-occupied mind of the long-distance cyclist, I was really looking forward to seeing the poster of the route at the control in Thirsk. You remember, the one with the colour photographs for each control, and the route laid out in its entirety from London to Edinburgh and back again. It would be good to see it again. The other thing I was looking forward to was that the total distance as far as Thirsk on the way south, as quoted in the route sheet, was exactly 1000 km.

It took about three and a half hours to do the 66 km to Thirsk, representing an average speed of just under 19km/h. In my planning, I was expecting to be riding at an average of 25km/h, whereas now, on day four, I thought I was doing pretty well to be cycling as fast as I was.

CHAPTER ELEVEN
You Need to Pace Yourself

One of the joys of cycling in an age of technology is that it is possible for your friends and family to track where you are. Every time we arrived at a control and reported in, our time was logged on the LEL website, and this information, our arrival time and the name of the latest control, was available on that website to anyone who knew your rider number.

My Good Lady had another facility available to her. Since I was carrying my phone, and since I could recharge it is with the dynamo on my bike, it was always turned on, she could track the location of my phone using her iPad. She found this quite exciting ("I'm enjoying this more than the Tour de France," she said, which is perhaps also a comment about the amount she enjoys televised cycle sport.) And she would often have her iPad on to watch my progress on Google Maps in real time. The fact that she'd engaged Junior with this activity is also a key reason why he was so impressed. Anything that happens on a computer is more exciting than something happening just in real life.

My mother — I didn't even know my mother was showing such a close interest — was following my progress through the website. And even she noticed I was slowing down after the third day. She and my uncle had conversations about this.

I was unaware of such monitoring. I had scarcely noticed I was even slowing down. But I was becoming more aware of the time limit. Normally when you have cycled 150 km in a day you are delighted to stop and feel you have earned a rest. This was not normally. In the middle of the afternoon of 31st August 2013, 150 km was not good enough, and there were more kilometres to fit into the day.

Alastair and Mario decided they needed a power nap. I was ready to go on, but I didn't think an hour's rest would do me any harm. We asked about such facilities at the Thirsk control once we'd taken on board the necessary food and drink.

"We've closed the gym now," the woman in the red T shirt told us apologetically.

"Oh."

"But I'm sure we can sort something out." She gave us directions to a hall, where the volunteers were packing the sleeping mattresses away into boxes. When we got there it was quiet, with the afternoon sunshine streaming through the windows. I could see four or five guys lying down on air beds. The young lady who was busily but quietly putting things away, no doubt towards the end of a very long shift, whispered to us that she was sorry it was so bright.

"It doesn't matter," we assured her.

"Do you want me to wake you?"

"In an hour, please," Mario said.

We lay down, pulling blankets over our sweaty cycling kit. I doubted I'd be able to sleep, but the next thing I knew, I was being woken by the gentle hand of a volunteer.

The rest probably helped: I was actually enthusiastic about getting back out onto the road. I wasn't the only one. Alistair, Mario, and I managed a remarkable minimum of faff and were moving again within twenty minutes of being woken.

It was warm, the sun was shining, and would continue to shine throughout the afternoon and early evening. We were cycling with a small group of other riders, members of which would change from time to time, so that we were generally surrounded by like-minded cyclists enjoying a shared experience, but after reasonable intervals there were new people to talk to.

Once again I was stronger than most of those around me when it came to riding uphill, but not otherwise, and I was no longer fit enough to leave Alistair behind. Not that I wanted to. I had had enough of cycling by myself.

We caught Becky after a while. Becky from Macclesfield as everybody called her on account of her Macclesfield Wheelers cycling jersey. I had seen her here and there over the last couple of days. She had been cycling with a couple of male clubmates to begin with, but had been struggling to keep up with them and had decided today that she would go at her own pace and was now enjoying that decision. I was enjoying conversation with her enough that I didn't mind Alistair and Mario moving ahead up the road, at least not for a few minutes.

"You're doing well," I said.

"I didn't expect to get further than Edinburgh," she said. "But when I got there, I thought I might as well keep going."

After a few minutes I told her I'd see her later, and, on an uphill stretch, cycled back up to Alistair, who teased me.

"Practising your technique?" he asked, mischievously. Meaning talking to women.

"Like I've got energy for that!"

One of the people I met was Peter Holland. We passed him a little later, just as we were coming into the Castle Howard stretch. Peter was riding a tricycle, the traditional kind with two wheels at the back, which is why I slowed down to talk to him. I always talk to tricyclists, asking them if they know my uncle. The world of tricycling is small enough that invariably they do.

Tricycles are not like bicycles. It's pretty obvious, but I thought I would point it out again. For one thing, the extra wheel gives extra rolling resistance, meaning that on a flat road, everything else being equal, they are significantly slower. The weight of the extra wheel, and of the extra frame material to accommodate it, and the rear differential necessary to drive to rear wheels, is a very significant factor when cycling uphill. In addition, they are less manoeuvrable, and require considerable skill to corner at speed, since it does not simply lean in the way a bicycle does. There are some reasons why a cyclist might choose to ride one, however. For somebody with balance problems, they are ideal, a way to cycle when a bicycle is not possible. If you are tired on a tricycle, and you stop, you can rest while sitting down. And, mostly important of all perhaps, they are different. They are full-on eccentric and for that reason I admire anybody who rides one.

Peter was a veteran of audax and endurance cycle rides, in particular 24-hour races, my uncle's favourite discipline. He spoke engagingly of his wife, to whom he was lucky to be married, who acted as his mission control on these events. She would be at home, monitoring his progress via the website, advising him on things like where he should rest, the distances ahead of him, and the food he should be eating. She had been telling him he was slowing down, and he needed to keep going to make the time control. For a man in his early 70s, he was pushing himself hard, and was coping with only one or two hours sleep a day, something he generally did in long-distance cycling events.

"Don't you ever fall asleep?" I said.

"I've done that twice," he said.

"Go on."

"One time, I woke up, and I noticed I was looking at stars where I was expecting the road to be. The other times I just rode into a hedge."

"I suppose that woke you up pretty quickly," I said.

Becky came past me while I was talking to Peter. After a while Peter urged me not to let my friends leave me behind by talking to him, and I excused myself and went on again.

I was really enjoying the cycling. Castle Howard, the monumental scale of all its mock castle features, and the remarkable landscape it was built on, was an exhilarating ride, and the fact that I'd seen it going the other way gave an enjoyable sense of anticipation as I approached each viewpoint.

I had another chat to Becky when I caught her up. She had spent time with Peter earlier in the day, and had picked up a lot of his life story, a life spent cycling. She thought it was sweet the way he spoke about his wife too.

I left Becky again and eventually caught Alistair and Mario before the stage flattened out, after which it would have been difficult for me to catch anyone. We cycled south towards Pocklington with the sun setting in the west, arriving at about 9:30.

While drinking the restorative mugs of tea, and eating heartily, we discussed our respective plans. Alistair and Mario were continuing to Market Rasen.

"I can't do that. I've learnt my lesson."

Alistair nodded.

But I knew I didn't have the luxury of time enough for a for a full night's sleep. When Becky arrived a few minutes later, she said she needed a few hours sleep and would then continue, and I thought it would be a good idea to accompany her. I didn't want to cycle at night on my own for fear of getting lost, and although cycling with Becky would be slower, I was less likely to get lost, and I would have some company.

I had a shower, and changed into the next day's cycling clothes, and then crawled under a blanket in the sports hall at the Pocklington control. The sports hall was as noisy and as smelly as ever, but I didn't need to bother with either ear plugs or meditation podcasts or even my sheet sleeping bag. I just slept.

And was woken at 2:30 as I had requested.

Actually, there was a bit of faff involved in getting myself to the sports hall to sleep. Most of that was finding the way to the showers, as they was in the different building. Finding things by walking around a school car park/playground after dark and with the brain turned zombie by lack of sleep and physical exhaustion seems to be an inexact science.

And waking up, there was still faff in my head. I felt like I was sleepwalking my way as I gathered things up and left the sports hall and went to the dining hall and provided myself with tea and muesli. And then having taken care of that business, it occurred to me that I hadn't seen Becky yet.

I knew she was up, because I had seen her heading out of the sports hall ten minutes earlier, too far ahead of me to speak to in a quiet environment. I had expected to see her in the dining room but when I didn't I went into autopilot breakfast mode. Slowly.

Now I looked outside, and found her bike by the entrance unlocked and ready to ride. A few moments later she was there too.

Somebody at the control gave us advice on the best way to get the Humber Bridge. In the middle of the night it made sense, apparently, to use the main road, since nobody else would be using it, instead of the country lanes described on the route sheet that might be harder to navigate in the dark.

So the plan was to cycle south out of Pocklington to catch the main A1079 road towards Hull. Then, near the town of Beverley, due north of the Humber Bridge, we would take the A164. It was a longer distance, but very much more straightforward. What could possibly go wrong?

It was a warm night, with only a slight headwind, and I was feeling good. We chatted about how acceptable it was to be obsessed by bicycles, and to how much of a degree you could get away with. She confessed she had got to the stage where she no longer thought about buying clothes unless they were made of either Gore-Tex or Lycra.

The road had a perfect surface, making a comfortable ride, and a quiet one, with only the sound of the wet tyres licking the wet road from rain we had missed. We chatted on the flat stages, and I waited for her at the top of climbs, and we enjoyed the width of the road on the long descents, tucked down out of the wind to roll further without effort.

It was taking us a long time to get to the bridge. I began to question the wisdom of taking a longer route to keep to the main roads, and then to make matters worse we missed the turning, following the signs to Hull instead of to the bridge. In my mind, the bridge went to Hull, which is not quite the geographical reality.

We tried to head cross-country to regain the right road. At one point we found a cycle path signposted Humber bridge, and thought we'd cracked it. And the cycle path began with a delightful descent along a narrow paved track filled with rabbits which ran this way and that out of the way of our lights and wheels.

"That was a bit like a video game," Becky said at the bottom.

Unfortunately rabbit games did not feature again, and the cycle path, like all too many cycle paths, was overly difficult to navigate, and we lost it after a few miles, needing to stop and consult Google Maps before we could continue.

The Humber Bridge is one of the engineering marvels of the world. For 16 years it was the longest suspension bridge anywhere on the planet, and although it is now relegated to seventh place, it is still the longest bridge you can cycle over. It is a political marvel also. The necessary funding was made available in 1966 when Prime Minister Harold Wilson's precarious government desperately needed to win the Hull North by-election, and the Minister of Transport Barbara Castle sanctioned the bridge. Nevertheless, it was another 15 years until the bridge was opened. For a long time, as well as being the longest suspension bridge on Earth, it was also the most expensive toll road in the country, a result of the huge cost of the bridge and the desire by the government to recover the necessary debt. The sharpest criticism of the bridge is that it links nowhere to nowhere: the bridge has relatively little traffic because there are no large population centres to the south of the estuary, and Hull to the north is not so very big either.

As we approached the bridge, on something of a circuitous route, we were becoming aware of the time. There were already signs of dawn to the east, and we were less than halfway through the stage, and the 12km/h schedule meant I needed to be at Market Rasen by just before eight o'clock.

"Go ahead," Becky said. "Don't let me hold you back." Becky had started half an hour after me, and so she was in less need of urgency; she also claimed to be less concerned about finishing within the time. She said she was happy to have reached Edinburgh and anything further was a bonus.

I didn't want to leave her behind. It didn't seem gentlemanly. On the other hand...

By the time I reached the bridge it was daylight, around about the same time of day as when I'd come the other way across. Once again I took it slowly, savouring the view. On the other side, finding myself once again among the small villages on the flat terrain south of the estuary, I met a man walking his dog at five in the morning.

"Been cycling far?"

"You could say that," I said.

"There were a lot of folk going the other way, a couple of days back," he said.

"I'm with them," I told him.

"They were going to Edinburgh."

"Now we're coming back."

"How far you going then?" he asked. And then when I told him, he said, "You're crazy," he said. Then, and to my surprise, he looked suddenly wistful, and said, "I'd love to do something like that."

I had remembered the hills leading up to the bridge on the way north, and I was prepared for them, and then when I reached them they weren't anything much, and any hardship caused by the gradient was almost compensated by a reduction in the headwind.

But I was pushing myself now, one eye on the clock. I wanted to arrive before eight. More specifically, before 8:04 a.m. I was pretty sure it didn't matter if you didn't make the time control on an intermediate stage, as long as you didn't miss it by too much, and as long as you had a reasonable chance of making the final control within the allotted time. Pretty sure, but not certain.

I did a decent job of catching up, but not quite good enough. I arrived at 8:06, lent the bike up against a wall near the entrance to Middlecot School where the control was, and rushed in, pulling my shoes off without bothering with the Velcro. At the desk, where three volunteers sat, two with paperwork and one with a laptop, nobody mentioned the minutes I was overdue. I didn't mention it them either, perhaps hoping that if nobody noticed I would get away with it.

CHAPTER TWELVE
The Hottest Day of the Year so Far

Market Rasen had a Day After feel about it. It was like a ghost town. Everybody had died, or they'd gone away. The riders anyway. The volunteers here were subdued, as if they hadn't yet come to terms with what had happened to everyone. Or they were very tired.

It was dark. It had been dark here on the way north. The school here was on the dark side, so to speak. The dark made it seem more like the aftermath of something.

There was nothing much to eat either. There was nobody behind the serving counter that had been so busy on Monday morning, and there was no food, no hot food at least, for them to serve. There were toasters, but there was nothing to put in them. What there was was muesli. There were jugs of some watery white liquid with froth on it, which I looked at several times before it occurred to me that this was some form of milk.

"What is this?" asked a heavy Italian accent.

I turned around. The voice belonged to a very striking young woman who looked very pissed off. I turned to look at her with my half asleep eyes.

She was certainly beautiful, with long flowing hair, perfect bronze skin, and big eyes, all that, and she might well have been a model. She looked disgusted with the food on offer, this place, the event, the whole thing, the way you might expect a top model to regard reconstituted dried milk in an empty cafeteria. She was wearing a white miniskirt, and white beach sandals, and a big loose cardigan rather than anything cycle specific, and I guessed she was somebody's girlfriend, she was here supporting her man

127

who was cycling, and she didn't know why she was here, what she was doing. To my mind she became that modern phenomenon, a footballer's wife.

"I think it's milk," I said.

She sniffed it suspiciously.

"I think they've made it with powder. I'm sure it's safe, if nothing else." I poured some of the unpleasant looking milk on my cereal and shuffled off to find a place in the dining room. I was keen to avoid this woman in case her bad mood was contagious.

There were 12 large circular empty tables and I chose one in the middle. I drank my tea and ate my muesli and I rearranged the the route sheet in the map pocket of my handlebar bag. I checked that there were no messages on my phone. A number of other individuals came in and sat on nearby tables, so there was a library study atmosphere to people eating muesli for breakfast.

At the corner of my eye I noticed a woman walking across the dining room to the exit. It was the same footballer's wife, only now she was wearing colourful Lycra and carrying a cycle helmet. I turned to stare at her as she walked outside, and stepped into her cycle shoes. I continued staring as she headed towards the bike racks and out of sight.

Back inside, a conversation had broken out. Two men sitting on adjacent tables were talking quietly about their experiences of the ride so far. One was John Spooner, who had famously (I mean famously within the community of riders who take part in events like LEL) completed all six previous LEL events, an achievement unique in human endeavours, and the other was Drew Buck, now dressed as a very much dishevelled French onion seller (or grape seller), and also, as I now understood, something of a legend amongst that same community of riders. They were talking quietly, but the semi-deserted dining room was even quieter. I listened intently, but it was like listening to the weather forecast; I was interested to hear what they had to say, but then afterwards I had little recollection of anything they had said.

"It's the night where we're going to lose it," I heard Drew say.

I remembered that line because I had been so busy thinking that today was the last day, that I had forgotten that my deadline was about six in the morning, and that the rate I had been going I was going to be riding until some time in the early hours.

It was already warming up by the time I set out for Kirton, and it was promising to be a glorious day, provided that you could stay out of the wind. The wind was strong and from the south, as it had been all week in Lincolnshire and Cambridgeshire. The landscape would go from gently undulating to pancake flat by the time we passed Woodhall Spa again, and any trees or hedgerows that could give shelter were few and far between.

I might have mentioned previously that I'm not a big fan of flat land. It is possible that I didn't mention it quite so forcefully on the early stages of the ride when the huge tailwind pushed us forwards on our adventure. It wasn't so thrilling then, but at least it was easy. Easy was no longer the case. Today, the last full day, would be hard into the headwind the whole time.

I found myself being quite enthralled by the small screen of my GPS unit. The big number there indicated my speed, and underneath it were displayed my average speed for the stage, and the time of day. In the flat landscape this passed for entertainment.

My speed hovered in the early 20s. The average was 19 point something kilometres per hour. I could not remember when it was that I had abandoned the notion of 25km/h during stages and 20km/h overall discounting sleeping time, but it was a long time ago. I did, however, hope to keep my moving average above 20km/h. So every time I looked at the GPS, I was motivated to increase the pressure my legs were putting on the pedals, to urge the number on the screen upwards, above 20, and each time I was successful, and the speed did increase, and I gritted my teeth to hold it there until the ache in my legs broke into my focus and I slowed down again.

I was cycling solo once more. There was no shortage of cyclists to meet and greet and briefly converse with, but all of them were either going too quickly for me to latch onto them, or they were going much slower than I would want to.

Finally there was a young man who caught up with me and then sat on my wheel for a minute or so, before pushing ahead.

He was only inching away, and I instinctively felt this was an opportunity, and I made my legs hurt and hurt in an effort to close the gap and to follow him. Immediately my speed, which had been hovering around 20km/h, went up to 24km/h. And for less effort.

So long as I remained in this young rider's wind shadow, it was significantly easier to maintain the speed. But the moment the gap between my front wheel and his rear increased beyond the few centimetres, it became harder. To stay in touch required some effort of concentration.

We covered a couple of kilometres like this, and I was beginning to wonder if my presence had been even noticed, when eventually he moved out towards the centre of the road and slowed down fractionally, inviting me to move up and fill the space.

I looked at him for the first time. His face, I mean. He was in his late 20s, had thick blonde hair and a decent, full face beard.

"Hi," I said.

"I'm Andrew," he said.

"Malcolm."

And with that flurry of conversation done with, I moved ahead and into the wind to do my share.

The screen of the GPS units became important again. I set myself a target of 23km/h and tried to hold to that, ignoring the pain in my legs. I also looked at the clock, noting it was 21 minutes past the hour, and deciding it would be reasonable to stay on the front for at least five minutes, so that immediately I was willing the number 26 to appear in the bottom right corner of the screen.

To those of you who think that cycling at 23km/h is not a particularly ambitious target for anybody on a decent road bike on a good road surface on level ground, no matter what the wind, I can only apologise. If you are looking for stronger stuff in your narrator all I can do is recommend some other books where you might find it.

Five minutes is actually quite a long time, long enough to cover nearly 2 km at the speed I was managing while I waited for each and every minute between 21 and 26 and kept up an ongoing internal dialogue as to whether I could relax yet or not.

The moment the clock moved from 1025 to 1026, I eased off on the pedals and moved to the right to let Andrew through. I sat on his wheel for the next couple of kilometres until he moved aside to let me come through again. We continued in this fashion, sometimes exchanging a word or two as we swapped places, but more often not. The wind took away all desire for conversation.

I was thirsty, but drinking was an issue. I carried one and a half litres of fluid in my two bottles, which wasn't quite enough to keep me hydrated over the 68 km of this stage, but it was slightly more than I was physically able to drink. There was no question of stopping to drink water, and every sip required that you lose some of your focus on cycling forwards. There was also the not insignificant task of removing the bottle from the bottle cage and bringing it to your mouth at a time when brain function seemed to be at a minimum. Having taken a sip of water, you needed to swallow it quickly to free the mouth up for the next breath of air, and that was also a task which now seemed difficult.

The stage went due south, skirting around the city of Lincoln, and the town of Boston, leaving me oblivious of either place until I looked closely at a map days later. I have never been to Lincoln nor to Boston, Lincolnshire (nor Boston Massachusetts either) and perhaps one day I will put that right. Or not.

After Woodhall Spa, we crossed the River Withem and then turned left along its course. Thereafter we had left the

Lincolnshire Wolds, and for the rest of this stage and the whole of the next one it would be totally flat.

The place names, entirely forgotten from the way north a few days ago, had words like Holland and Fen in them, and on one occasion both, to indicate the state of the landscape. Wherever there was a bridge, it was such a remarkable feature that it had a name.

We continued, Andrew and I, taking our turns on the front. My turns were consistently exactly 5 minutes, with the speed of no more than 23km/h but only very rarely less than this. Andrew generally managed 23.5 or 24km/h and lasted up to 7 minutes. Once he said, "it's definitely easier with two of us."

"It is," I agreed, delighted that he thought so. It was definitely easier for me.

Easier, but not easy. Not at all easy.

Kirton is sometimes known as Kirton-in-Holland. Those of us unfamiliar with Lincolnshire are perhaps unaware that Holland is a part of that county and has been since mediaeval times. The area is extremely low-lying, with a maximum altitude of 5 m, if you can use the word altitude in such a situation, and this 5 m is only achieved on artificially built levees, so that drainage is a big issue. It reminds you a bit of the other Holland, but the two names, apparently, have different origins. The Lincolnshire Holland means "land of the hill spurs," although to my recollection the hill spurs are more remarkable for their absence. The word Holland also refers to a region of the Netherlands properly, although most people use it as a synonym for the country's name. It is derived from the Middle Dutch term "holds land", which means wooded land, according to the Oxford English Dictionary, despite a popular idea that it comes from a contraction of "hollow land", a description of its low-lying geography.

Whatever the derivation of the word Holland, Andrew and I arrived at the Kirton control, the Middlecott School, just after 1230 in the afternoon.

There wasn't much faff at Kirton, partly because I had the urge to finish this thing now, in part because I wanted to keep up with Andrew. By the time I'd parked my bike and taken my shoes and helmet off, and registered at the control, and gone to the toilet, and found the dining room, Andrew was already sitting down with his meal. I joined him as fast as I could, and found him talking to the footballer's wife. The footballer's wife who was actually a footballer herself. I mean cyclist. And she didn't look pissed off this time. They were talking about the sunshine and the distance they had travelled, and Andrew was saying he felt good and the footballer's wife was saying she did too, and then she was saying see you later, and she was heading out.

"I'm feeling really good," Andrew said again, when she was gone.

"I'm feeling okay," I said, hesitantly. It was the best I could do.

"I wanted to finish on Thursday."

"That was my plan too." At 25km/h etc etc.

All too quickly we were back outside, filling water bottles, strapping helmets on and getting on with it. Immediately we were back into the chain gang routine, me doing five minutes exactly on the front, and Andrew doing a little bit more, a little bit faster.

He was feeling good, I could see it in his face every time we swapped over. And he was enjoying himself, the bastard. I just clung on to his wheel, hoping it would be over, if not soon then soon enough.

At least I was on schedule. While I was cycling with Andrew I was on schedule. Having arrived at Market Rasen eight minutes behind, we'd got to Kirton with half an hour in hand. If I could continue this kind of pace I could arrive in Loughton with a couple of hours to spare.

Increasingly, however, I was becoming aware that I could not keep up with Andrew.

It was getting hotter. In fact it was the hottest day of the year thus far, and in this part of the country it would reach 32°C. It was like cycling in a fan oven, and towards the fan. But Andrew

133

was managing 24km/h into the wind and I could barely hold his wheel, and when I was on the front I was struggling to get close to this speed. One time Andrew overtook me before my five minutes was up in his impatience to keep the pace up. I put a renewed effort into my next turn on the front, and managed the full five minutes, then when I moved aside to let him through, I was unable to prevent myself drifting backwards away from him and could only watch him power up the road into the wind.

On my own again, my speed dropped to 18 or so kilometres per hour. By the time Andrew noticed I was no longer there, I was probably half a mile behind. He didn't wait for me. I wouldn't have waited for me.

I did maths in my head. I had done 21 km in less than an hour, there were 60 km left and at my current speed that would be another three hours and 20 minutes. Allowing for a couple of decent breaks I would still be at St Ives in four hours, less than five hours for the stage, and I would still be within my schedule, albeit by a small margin. It was okay, I could relax a little.

I wasn't enjoying this. I wasn't enjoying the heat, the wind, or the pain. I wasn't enjoying the scenery. I told myself I would have a break at Crowland, where I'd stopped at the shop on the way up, and I enjoyed counting down the kilometres before I arrived.

At one point the route sheet told me to turn right off the B1173 but the road was blocked, with signs indicating a diversion on account of some kind of essential work being carried out. The blockade was so professionally done I needed to get off the bike to negotiate it. Thereafter I had a beautifully empty traffic free road to enjoy. After a mile I passed the point where a drainage ditch was being renovated, with heavy machinery blocking three quarters of the road, and a little after that I saw Drew Buck having a wash in a stream a little way back from the road.

I met John Spooner a while later, after I had rejoined the B1173. He was riding steadily, a little slower than me, and conversation would be a welcome distraction for a while.

"You look like you've done this before," I said, as if I didn't know, by way of starting a conversation. He did, too, he had an

134

easy pace, and looked like he was enjoying himself. His bicycle was a traditional looking machine but made in titanium and with a decent spread of gears, and dynamo lighting. He was wearing sandals with SPD fittings.

"I have indeed."

"How many times have you done this ride?"

"Six. Seven if I finish."

"We're nearly there, aren't we?"

"No need to tempt fate."

"You must enjoy it."

"I do that. Some bits I enjoy more than others, though. I wouldn't choose to go through the Fens."

We were cycling along the bank beside the River Welland, and at this point you could actually see the river, and it was pretty.

"I'm expecting to see Drew Buck soon," John said. "He set off five minutes before me, and I was expecting to catch him up before now."

I told him where I'd seen Buck, and John told me he'd gone round the diversion, knowing it wasn't any greater distance to travel.

I cycled with John for a couple of kilometres before moving ahead. I was feeling a little better now, and, significantly, I was approaching an ice cream stop.

Approaching Crowland, there was a long straight section of road lined with mature willow trees I remembered from the route north, and now, as I passed them cycling the other way, I could see, in the shadow of many of the trees, a sleeping cyclist. The shade of a willow tree was almost irresistible, and if it wasn't for my GPS unit telling me it was only a couple of kilometres until the shop in Crowland, I would have stopped.

At the shop, there were a couple of bicycles parked outside, and a cyclist enjoying a 99. A German cyclist came out of the shop with a can of Coke and a can of orange Fanta, and he proceeded to mix the two of them in his water bottle.

"What are you doing?" I asked him. A strange question, considering I could see what he was doing. I really meant, *why are you doing that?*

"In Germany we do this all the time." I had been able to tell he was German because of the label on his bike. "You can even buy it ready mixed, it's called Spezi."

I didn't fancy it. It sounded disgusting and still sounds disgusting to me, but then I am not a soft drink fan. It was ice cream I had stopped for, although I bought some water as well, aware that I had already started my second water bottle and I was less than halfway through the 81 km stage.

Armed with my choc ice of choice, I picked up my bike and rode it the 500 m to the monument, because this was where I had decided I was going to enjoy my rest break.

Andrew was sitting on a bench outside the pub opposite the monument, halfway through a half pint of beer. He clearly *was* feeling good. I sat down next to him.

Crowland was built around Croyland Abbey, and had nothing whatsoever to do with crows. Originally the Abbey had been built on an island in the Fens where St Gundlach had chosen to live as a hermit. As the Abbey developed, the nearby marshlands were drained, and the town grew up nearby.

"Do you know what it is?" I asked.

"I think it's some kind of bridge," Andrew said.

The monument that Andrew and I were looking at is Trinity Bridge, so-called because it was constructed as a three sided bridge which crossed the River Welland at its confluence with the River Withem, giving access to three places separated by water from a single bridge. The current lack of any water underneath it made it difficult for the uninformed observer to decide its original function.

The bridge was built in stone by monks from the Abbey sometime in the 14th century, although there was some kind of triangular bridge on the site in 943 A.D. The drainage of the Fens, and the diversion of rivers, have now left it stranded on dry land.

Once we had finished with our respective refreshments, we set off again together. The rest had done me good, either that or half a pint of beer had slowed Andrew down sufficiently, and I was now able to keep up, and we maintained a decent pace for the next 20 km. Somewhere along the way we picked up Tim Trickedem Decker, so there were now three of us battling into the wind.

From Crowland we had been following the B1040 towards St Ives, and by afternoon this road had become busy with traffic in both directions. Although the traffic made cutting our way through the wind easier, it made for a very uncomfortable ride, especially with overtaking cars giving us only a few inches of safety margin as they passed.

About two hours after we had left Crowland, there was the sound of a siren from somewhere behind. One of the emergency services. The siren got closer, as whatever vehicle it was forced its way through the traffic.

"I got a bad feeling about this," Tim said.

"Let's just hope it's nothing to do with us," Andrew said. Meaning nothing to do with the event, with cyclists.

It was an ambulance, and it passed us a minute or so after we first heard it, and made its way forward up the road past cars which had pulled over to the side to allow it.

A few minutes later we could see the flashing light of the ambulance a few hundred metres up the road. We approached with a sense of trepidation. A driver coming the other way, window wound down, shouted at us:

"Single file! Don't you guys ever learn?"

Or something like that. Something irrelevant and ignorant and emotive shouted on a baking hot day by somebody stuck in traffic. But it told us whatever had happened was definitely about a cyclist or cyclists.

And when we got there it was Peter Holland. He was lying on the road just in front of the ambulance, his head resting on the curb, a paramedic kneeling in front of him, and Peter's tricycle on the pavement. There were two or three bystanders gathered, and an LEL cyclist, and I imagined one of these had called the ambulance. There was a line of blood making its way down Peter's face and he looked in shock, but his eyes were open.

Tim was animated, telling the paramedic about crazy car drivers, and the paramedic, only a young man, was very politely calming him down. "According to the people here, there was no car involved."

It became clear to me that Peter had fallen asleep. The only car involved was the parked one he had ridden into.

Tim and Andrew rode on, but I told them I wanted to stay for a few moments. I wanted to speak to Peter, ask if I could pass on a message, something like that. I wanted to see that he was okay. I loitered for a few minutes, but it was clear he wasn't going to recognise me or tell me anything especially coherent. I heard him say, "this is all silly." I got the impression he was going to be okay, but that he would not be cycling the rest of the way to London. I gave the trike a look over. The outside rear wheel was badly buckled, and the right hand brake lever was scratched and out of alignment, but other than that it looked okay. I thought he had probably hit the outside of the car, and bounced outwards into the road, folding his outside wheel under him. It was fortunate that any driver behind him had managed to stop in time.

I figured there was nothing I could do that wasn't already being done by other people, and decided to go on.

But I was on my own again now, making my own way into the wind. I was back to 18km/h and working hard to do it. And I was no longer in the mood.

My legs ached. My knee was sore. I was tired from lack of sleep, and fed up with the day's headwind. I was thinking about Peter, and his wife at home. And my knee was sore.

Twenty-five years ago an old man drove a Mercedes-Benz into my right knee cap. It was early evening, and I had been cycling home from work. I was wearing a fluorescent yellow jacket and had decent working lights, and the road was well lit, and the driver of the Mercedes didn't see me, and turned right across my path. The driver was very polite and apologetic, and it later turned out he wasn't insured, the car was not registered in his name, and the police were unable to trace him. My bike was replaced under my insurance, and I managed to get compensation from some kind of Uninsured Driver Scheme, but my knee has suffered intermittent problems ever since. Sometimes it stiffens up after a hard ride, sometimes I twist it while running or walking or swimming or turning over in bed, and it always gives me trouble if I don't keep it warm, necessitating a knee pad if I am wearing shorts on anything but a hot day. Once I had to curtail a cycle-camping tour of southern Turkey because of it, and I often need to give it a couple of day's rest.

Now my knee was hurting. When I thought about it, and it was demanding attention now, it was hurting a lot. This was more serious than being tired, and more serious than the usual aches and pains. This could be the end of my ride.

I needed to stop and assess the situation. I decided I would find a decent place, and walk up and down for a bit, hoping against hope that my knee would then settle down.

Soon enough I found a layby, where a path led into the woods. I stopped, and climbed off the bike. I had a pee, then I walked around for a moment. I stood on my left leg and carefully bent and unbent my right knee, and thus confirmed that this knee was very painful indeed.

In my handlebar bag was a packet of dried fruit I picked up the day before from my bag drop at Pocklington. I needed something like that to cheer me up. Unfortunately, with sweaty hands, and wearing a pair of cycling mitts, it wasn't easy to open. I didn't seem to be able to get a grip on it enough to tear it open. And at this point a wasp chose to land on the fingers of my right hand.

If it wanted the fruit, I thought, irritated, I hadn't even opened the packet!

Perhaps as frustrated with my ability to open it as I was, the wasp stung me, twice, just as it occurred to me that it might do so.

I am allergic to wasp stings.

I cursed and swore and shook my hands in the air and stamped my feet and the wasp flew off somewhere. I noticed that in the middle of all this drama I had actually succeeded in opening the packet of fruit.

I'm not allergic to the extent that I will suffer a heart attack, but generally if I suffer a wasp sting, or a bee sting, the affected part of me swells up grossly, and then I get feverish and confused and I have the worst headaches I ever get. Usually I get myself to hospital and have an injection of antihistamine and/or adrenaline, which sorts me out again.

I ate some of the dried fruit I had worked so hard for, while I came up with a plan of action. My uncle had recently recounted an incident when he had been stung by a bee just before a bike race and he didn't have his EpiPen with him. He'd cycled home to get it, going as fast as he could, and then found when he arrived that he no longer needed it because his body had manufactured the necessary adrenaline. Now I needed to do the same. I got back on the bike and peddled towards St Ives as if my life depended upon it.

I felt a rising panic, and I allowed myself to feel it, knowing that the panic was what was producing the adrenaline. I couldn't afford to think about my knee now, and I ignored the pain it gave me. I was pounding on the pedals, my speed now up to 25km/h, my heart thumping so hard I felt I could hear it. As I pushed myself forwards, I was also trying to concentrate on the route sheet, trying to read the next instructions as the words vibrated with the handlebars. Right at the left-hand bend, signposted Ramsey. I couldn't afford to stop at a junction to find my way, I had to keep moving.

I kept pushing. The panic was exciting, thrilling. I was enjoying it. I could barely feel the throbbing from my hand for the pain in my legs and in my lungs and that was good. There is good pain and bad pain. The pain from exertion is good and pain from injury is bad. This was good.

I had 15 km to go before St Ives when I had stopped. Now it was 10 km. Now it was five. Now it was turning left at the T-junction and I was entering the town.

I arrived at the control at St Ivo School on a wave of adrenaline, feeling like I was on a drug high. I went in, removing my shoes, helmet and gloves in the habitual manner, and presented myself at the check-in desk, and realised I couldn't even tell where I had been stung.

My knee wasn't hurting either.

It was 7:40 when I arrived, a good hour and 20 minutes ahead of schedule, but by the time I had met Andrew again, and had recounted to him, breathlessly, all that had happened to me in the last 20 km of the stage, and I calmed down a little, I realised I was dead tired. Conscious that I didn't want to fall asleep and cycle into a parked car, I decided I should take a short nap before I went any further.

The sleeping area at St Ives, or at least the sleeping area they were using at the time when I arrived, was a classroom rather than a sports hall. Of course the demand here, not much over 100 km from the start and finish, was never going to fill a sports hall. The room was completely cleared of furniture except for about a dozen inflatable mattresses, just over the half of them occupied by an unconscious cyclist. One of the unconscious was Alistair, I was delighted to see.

Even crashed out, and fast asleep, he looked neatly dressed in his Dulwich Paragon attire. I took the bed opposite. There was no question of washing, and I had no clean clothes to change into anyway, and I lay down and pulled a blanket over me.

I was only half asleep when Alistair was woken.

"Good to see you," he said, when I opened my eyes.

"Good to see you."

"I'm absolutely wrecked."

"You've been saying that the whole way," I joked. "See you at the finish."

For a moment I thought about getting up and cycling the rest of the way with him. It would have been nice, but I had closed my eyes and I drifted back to sleep again before I really finished the thought.

CHAPTER THIRTEEN
Getting to the End

I was woken at 9 o'clock, and made my way to the dining hall where I revived myself with tea, ate some muesli, and made myself some sandwiches. The sandwiches were a new idea: I realised that the more I could eat whilst I was cycling, the less time I needed for eating at the controls.

I felt good for having rested, and even better knowing there were only 120km remaining in front of me, eight hours to do it in.

It was just starting to get dark as I left, and pleasantly warm. Two other cyclists were just leaving, and I asked if I could join them.

"Sure thing," said the woman I had been thinking of as the footballer's wife. Her name was Francesca. The other was Calvin, a broad shouldered cheerful-looking young man. As we peddled up the road together, looking for the first right-hand bend 100m along, we came to an important realisation.

"There's no wind!"

I had been looking forward to this stage all day, because I knew that there were hills in it, which would be such a relief after the monotony of the flat Fens, but also would give shelter from the wind. And now there was no wind!

We spent a few minutes negotiating our way out of St Ives, failing to find directions for the town bridge. Calvin and I spent some time rereading the route sheet and looking at Google Maps before Francesca asked somebody, the group of us thus conforming to popular sexual stereotype.

We cycled through Fenstanton, the name meaning a fenland stone enclosure, and the town dating back to a Roman site built as a measure to combat Boadicea's tribesman. The village marked for us the end of the Fens, and shortly afterwards we climbed to an altitude of 10m for the first time in 24 hours, and then 50m as we climbed Crow Hill to the new town of Camborne, a settlement designed for 10,000 people and built from the late 90s onwards on what was previously farmland. The name of the town is taken from that of Cambridge, 14km to the east, and the nearby village of Born.

From the first, Calvin was having trouble on the climbs. He had hurt his neck, so that it was painful for him every time he used his upper body. At first he'd been struggling to look down at his route sheet, reading it with his head torch, so I told him to turn the head torch off and not to bother with the route sheet or navigation; Francesca and I could do that. But that didn't help him with the hills. We cycled through Born, and Great Evanston and Haslingfield, where Queen Elizabeth the First lost a ring. On the steep bump of Chapel Hill we left Calvin behind.

After we dropped him and waited for him a couple of times, we decided the third time not to wait. I felt guilty once again, as I did every time I didn't wait for somebody, but not guilty enough to make a difference.

Francesca and I cycled on.

I thought of Calvin as we passed the railway station at Shepreth (the small village was listed as Esceprid in the Doomsday book – the name means sheep stream – and it was a place where sheep could be washed on their final trip to Cambridge market) and then I didn't think of him again.

Francesca was cycling without a front light. She had three front lights attached to various places on her handlebars but none of them were turned on.

"Only one of them works," she explained, "and I need to save the battery."

Her rear light was working, for what it was worth, although for anyone behind her its light was probably obscured by her bulging saddle pack. We were cycling through rolling, wooded country, with steep descents and sharp turns, and she was riding ahead of me. I wondered if she had excellent night vision or if she was crazy.

"You're crazy!" I told her, having made up my mind. I had to peddle hard on the downhills to make sure I kept up with her since it was my light she was using.

Francesca was new to audaxing, and to long-distance cycling in general. "My friends, they said why not come with us and cycle from London to Edinburgh and back. I said sure, why not? I didn't know where is Edinburgh."

"You know now," I said.

"Yes," she laughed. "Now I know."

"But you're still riding."

"Yes. I was only going to Edinburgh and then stop, but when I am at Edinburgh, I think why not go further, and see how far I can."

"You've done very well," I said, "if you've never cycled this far before."

"Normally I do triathlons." She had run a marathon as well, and listening to her talking about her sport I got the idea she was pretty good at it, somebody who competes with the idea of winning events rather than simply completing them. Nobody gets on a bike and cycles a thousand kilometres in a week without having a pretty good level of general fitness.

I told her about my footballer's wife theory. She laughed. She disabused me of my idea that she'd been elegantly dressed; she had been wearing her scruffy jumper and had a towel wrapped around her waist. Remembering as far back as that morning, I realised this was true, but to my sleep-deprived eyes it had looked different.

We continued. I noticed that when an oncoming car appeared, she would turn on her front light, and then turn it off as soon as the car had gone. Most of the time we cycled side-by-side, so she could see perfectly well by my light, it was only when the road dropped downhill she tended to go on in front.

Near Fowlmere, where appropriately enough there is an RSPB site, and where the infamous Fen Tiger has been seen, we stopped to check a signpost at a junction at the top of a hill and noticed the light of a cyclist catching us up. For a moment we wondered if it was Calvin catching us up, having found another burst of energy, but we quickly realised it could not be. This was Andy.

Andy was a much more typical audax rider, a man in his 50s with half a lifetime of cycling behind him, most of it in cycling clubs. He had plenty of stories to tell, and was more than happy to share them. He was less interesting to talk to than Francesca was, but I didn't seem to have the choice. He was friendly and chatty, and seemed happy to have somebody to listen to his stories. I didn't want to tell him to shut up. Francesca dropped back now, following a few bike lengths behind.

It was after midnight now, cooling off just a little, and we stopped to put on extra layers. The moon was up, making a perfect night for cycling. We continued, the road very smooth under our wheels.

Audley End House is described by Wikipedia as one of the finest Jacobean houses in England. Basically a palace, it is set back in its own extensive gardens that were landscaped by Capability Brown. It was a magnificent sight in the moonlight.

"That looks a nice place to stay the night," I said.

Andy agreed. "They should have a room to spare, at least."

I didn't recognise it as Audley End House at the time, but I would have done had I memorised the appropriate instruction on the route sheet. So by the time we'd cycled another mile or so, and I'd listened to Andy recounting yet another of his long-distance-ride-followed-by-pub-session, I wondered aloud if we had missed a turning.

"Now that you mention it...."

We stopped and examined the instructions by torchlight. We should have taken the left-hand turning signposted Audley End House.

"I think I know where that is." I said.

After we had backtracked, we cycled through Debden and Cutters Green – the cutters in question being those who cut the grass for thatched roofs –and Thaxted — a place where thatch was got – without incident, but not without admiring these pretty villages with their thatched cottages. And then we came to Great Easton.

Great Easton is a small village dating from the 12th century. It has a population of just a few hundred people, one pub, one church, and one Rolls-Royce dealership. The control was in the village hall, where a huge spread of food lay on a set of tables running along the middle of the hall, with chairs for a hundred or so around the outside. Francesca, Andy and I sat at the table.

After the first cup of tea Francesca went away to shower, while Andy and I were taking on board more calories, and we were still doing that when she came back wearing her "elegant" cardigan, her hair wrapped in a towel, and a fresh pair of cycling shorts. She intended to get some sleep before cycling the last 45 km back to Leighton, completely unconcerned about finishing within her time limit. For her, riding to Edinburgh and back was achievement enough, and why shouldn't it be?

We said our goodbyes, and Andy and I faffed and then shuffled our way back onto our bikes and into the night. There was no hurry, we had three hours to cycle 45 km on a windless, moonlit night over gently undulating terrain. The route was simple, and, according to one of the volunteers, every junction was signposted. It felt like a formality.

We passed through Great Dunmow, whose name means "meadow on the hill", originally the site of a Roman settlement on Stane Street. The region ranked as the fourth best rural location to live in the UK, according to the local district council. At three in the morning, it was very pretty at least.

Andy recounted some more of his audax adventures, and then started talking about a bicycle frame he'd had built. I pointed out that Venus had just risen to the east, ahead of the sun, and successfully diverted the conversation for a couple of minutes.

We passed High Roding, Aythorpe Roding, and Leaden Roding, three of a group of villages, apparently the largest group of villages bearing a common name in the country, the remnants of a single Anglo-Saxon village set up by a character named Hroda. The full list of Rodings includes Beauchamp, Berners, Margaret, and White, as well as Abbess Roding, which we would have cycled through had we not missed the turn.

Andy was telling me how successful his new bicycle had been on a tour of northern England last year when it dawned on me that we had been merrily peddling our way along the A1064 for a long while without being troubled by a junction.

We stopped, and consulted Google Maps, to realise we were definitely in the wrong place. We had spent 20 minutes cycling at a reasonable pace in a direction at right angles to the one we needed, thus getting no closer to our destination. We were only about 25 km from Loughton, but the direct route there looked complicated, something that would be difficult to navigate. I decided the most sensible course of action would be to retrace our steps most of the way, until a suitable right-hand turn in would deliver us onto the original route.

Suddenly I was desperately short of time. For Andy, this was less of a problem, because he had set off on the Sunday a whole hour later than me and had that hour in hand.

We doubled back, and I set the pace. I couldn't be sure how many kilometres it would now take us to get to Loughton, and therefore couldn't be sure what speed was necessary.

At White Roding, the right-hand turn was into a narrow looking lane, and I had already decided, looking at Google Maps in-flight, that it would be quicker to continue backtracking to the junction we had missed, signposted Fyfield.

I wanted to pace myself, but it was difficult to do that without knowing what minimum pace was necessary.

"You don't want to overdo it," Andy told me, shouting from behind my wheel.

"I don't want to underdo it either."

It was getting light, gradually, but I didn't welcome it. The coming daylight merely served as a reminder that my time was running out. The time limit might be an entirely arbitrary idea, without real significance, but unlike Francesca I did care about it. And I didn't intend to miss it.

The next junction appeared, one I hadn't noticed on the map, but it was a decent road, pointing in the right direction, and I didn't feel I had the option to ignore it.

"I'm going this way," I shouted.

I was aware that I needed to keep calm, not panic, and to get the navigation right. It wasn't easy, however, as the scale on my map, cut out from the road atlas, was too small to show the relevant country lanes, and it was still too dark to read the route sheet easily, and Google Maps took ages to load. And my mental state, with one hour of sleep in the last 24, didn't make it any easier.

In fact by now I was back on the route, but I was unaware of this. We were on a long country road, without signposts for a while, so I had no way of confirming I was doing the right thing. What I desperately wanted was to know where I was and exactly how many kilometres I had left to complete before 5:55 a.m.

The route sheet also had two options here, a daytime route negotiating lots of pretty country lanes, and a more straightforward B-road route. These options only served to confuse.

"I'm sorry to say this, "Andy said, drawing level with me for a moment, "but I need a crap."

"Right."

"I just need to find the right place."

I kept cycling, keeping the pace up, 25km/h showing on my GPS, the screen now visible in the twilight.

"I'm good at this," he said. "I've got it down to a tee."

It was gone five in the morning, and I had less than an hour to go.

"This will do."

An open gate, leading into a farmer's field. Andy slowed down, and pulled in. "I won't be long."

"I'm not stopping," I shouted.

I didn't even slow down.

There was a signpost for Toot Hill, a location that was printed in bold on the route sheet, meaning it was a location we actually cycled through, so I took that. A little later, I came to the village of Ongar, and then a left turn signposted Toot Hill, which had an LEL route arrow affixed to it. I knew where I was. The route sheet told me this was 31.3 km into the stage, and I quickly worked out that meant I had 14.6 km left to cover.

At this point I had just over half an hour left, so I needed an average speed of 30km/h, having been pushing myself to make 23km/h for the last hour.

I knew where the goalposts were now, and it was easy to summon the necessary adrenaline. 30km/h duly appeared on the GPS, then 31, 32. My thighs were full of pain, but the pain seemed to help my focus. Right at the next junction, then left. I had gone through two junctions without pausing, or even paying much attention to the possibility of a car coming the other way. I made a mental note that it would be a poor idea to have an accident.

The road ran parallel with the M11 for a stretch, a few cars already driving into the city at this time in the morning. I crossed the M25, a clear sign I was close to home.

I was continuing to do mental arithmetic as I rode, notwithstanding the struggle I had with this in my sleep-deprived state. 6 km left, 12 minutes. Most of the time the GPS showed 31 or 32km/h, but then there were junctions, and uphill sections, where it went right down. It was touch and go.

It was a beautiful morning. I passed another cyclist, then another, each time struggling to shout "Good morning!" while maintaining the necessary speed. I passed John Spooner, who was gently trundling his way towards his seventh successful LEL ride. The cyclists I passed all had plenty of time in hand.

I passed an LEL signpost marked

ONLY 3 KM TO GO!

At my current speed that meant six minutes, and I had 10 minutes remaining. Suddenly I knew I was going to make it.

There were signs for 2 km and 1 km, and indeed, signs on the junctions which were much easier to see in the full light of morning. Just as well, because it meant I could keep my speed up, not having to slow down to think about the junctions.

I rolled into the familiar entranceway to Davenant School at 5:50, negotiating the path marked in temporary barriers to the control. I parked my bike against the wall and checked the time again. I had four minutes left. I waited for a moment, breathing deeply, recovering my composure. I considered waiting another few minutes, to approach the control point in the dying seconds of my allotted time, but realised there was a very real chance that I might miscalculate. I went inside to get the last stamp on my card.

"Cutting it a bit fine, aren't you?" the man behind the laptop said.

"Tell me about it."

I surrendered my now-completed Brevet card, which had to be sent away for certification or something, and was presented with the rather glorious LEL medal, with the date on one side, and an outline of Great Britain made up of the names of all the controls on the other. Then Damon Peacock interviewed me, as he was interviewing all finishers for his video. And when I was finished with that I sat down on a step and concentrated on breathing. The interview appears in Damon's film of the event, available via his website, www.damonpeacock.com.

Other finishers came in, the ones I'd passed at speed on the approach to Loughton, and they got their medals and were interviewed. John Spooner merited a longer interview.

After about fifteen minutes, Andy arrived.

Andy and John Spooner knew each other, and they started to chat, and I let their conversation drift over me until Andy was mentioning somebody he had been cycling with, who hadn't waited when he needed the toilet, and who had been struggling to meet the time limit.

"I hope he's arrived already," Andy said, "I tried to find him afterwards, and cycled as fast as I could, but he didn't wait for me."

"I wasn't waiting for anybody!" I said.

They looked down, and laughed. I stood up to join the conversation.

"I tried to catch you up," Andy said.

"There's no way you would have caught me," I told him.

He assured me that he had been no more than 45 seconds in the field, as it were, and that he would have been able to help me keep my speed up.

"I'm glad you got here though," he said, "if you had arrived now, out of time, I would have to hide."

I got myself some tea, and something to eat, and I drank the tea and ate the something, and got some more tea and drank that and then there wasn't really very much more to do. The dining hall that had been full of expectation and excitement just five days ago was mostly empty and mostly quiet. What conversations there were went on in low voices. On the far side of the room were two rows of mattresses where a number of people slept and snored. A couple of red-shirted volunteers were busy packing things away. It was the end of the event. Most of the riders had either arrived and already made their way home or to the hotel or the campsite, or they had given up; few were left out on the road.

I wasn't ready to leave, but I couldn't see any reason to stay. Somehow it was already approaching 7 o'clock in the morning and the city would be busying itself and I decided if I were going home now I had better get a move on.

There was no question of cycling all the way home. No question of another 30 km being nothing after 1400 km. I was going to cycle to the nearest railway station, which was Chigwell, take a train to central London, and then cycle to Waterloo, and take the train from there. And I wasn't enthusiastic about cycling to Chigwell.

Chigwell was about 6 km away, and I needed to stop half a dozen times to check my directions on the way. The train I caught was busy with commuters already, and I was lucky to get my bike onto it. Having achieved this, I was less lucky in finding myself a place to sit, and had to stand all the way to Liverpool Street. Standing did not prevent me from falling asleep on and off throughout the short journey.

I needed coffee at Liverpool Street, and a pasty, and hoped that with this additional fortification I would be able to get across the city at rush hour while remaining conscious. I wasn't convinced I would be able to, but nevertheless I wobbled off, uncertainly, into the traffic.

And then fortunately, and I do mean fortunately, there was a crack of thunder and the rain came down. Commuters produced umbrellas and battled their way through it. I let the cold rain wash over my face and laughed. By the time I reached Waterloo all the parts of me not covered in Gore-Tex were soaked to the skin but that was okay. I would be home in half an hour.

CONTROL 🍽🛏	N		S	
LOUGHTON	0	0	45	1418
GT EASTON	-	-	73	1373
ST IVES	99	99	81	1300
KIRTON	81	180	66	1219
MARKET RASEN	66	246	90	1153
POCKLINGTON	90	336	63	1063
THIRSK	65	401	67	1000
BARNARD CASTLE	67	468	82	933
BRAMPTON	82	550	57	851
MOFFAT	74	624	-	-
ESKDALEMUIR	-	-	47	794
TRAQUAIR	-	-	42	747
EDINBURGH	81	705		

Afterwards

To our modern way of thinking, 12km/h seems slow, but it is fast enough to get you anywhere you want to go. It seems to me that a sense of direction and a sense of purpose are far more useful than speed. At an average speed of 12km/h you can travel 240 km in a day. People routinely do this kind of distance by train or car and don't think anything of it, and then after a short period of time they travel the reverse distance in an equally short time. But in travelling like this, the places in between mean nothing. Have you really travelled, if you have seen nothing of the places along the way?

At an average speed of 12km/h you can cover a thousand kilometres in just over four days. At this speed you could travel all the way around the world in less than six months. At half that speed, or at a quarter that speed, you could make the same journey more realistically, with time to relax, and the ability to take days away from the bike, or to have time in reserve. That's as far as most people would ever dream of travelling in a lifetime.

Perhaps the message to me, that I have gained from taking part in this adventure, is a reminder of what is possible. I may not cycle around the world. I may not want to. But I could, and there are so many other things I can do provided I have the imagination, and can keep a sense of direction and a sense of purpose.

Check in History

Location	Time
Started	Sunday 09:15:00
St Ives	Sunday 13:16:42
Kirton	Sunday 17:10:03
Market Rasen	Sunday 20:57:45
Pocklington	Monday 09:17:45
Thirsk	Monday 13:18:03
Barnard Castle	Monday 17:57:36
Brampton	Monday 22:59:23
Moffat	Tuesday 08:54:39
Edinburgh	Tuesday 13:39:17
Traquair	Tuesday 18:15:36
Eskdalemuir	Tuesday 21:17:59
Brampton	Wednesday 01:34:03
Barnard Castle	Wednesday 11:29:58
Thirsk	Wednesday 15:45:45
Pocklington	Wednesday 21:20:11
Market Rasen	Thursday 08:06:11
Kirton	Thursday 12:33:35
St Ives	Thursday 18:41:06
Great Easton	Friday 01:54:27
London Loughton	Friday 05:51:24

Printed in Great Britain
by Amazon